ELECTING THE PRESIDENT

Adam C. Breckenridge

UNIVERSITY
PRESS OF
AMERICA

LANHAM • NEW YORK • LONDON

Copyright © 1982 by

University Press of America,™ Inc.

4720 Boston Way
Lanham, MD 20706

3 Henrietta Street
London WC2E 8LU England

Library of Congress Cataloging in Publication Data

Breckenridge, Adam Carlyle, 1916–
    Electing the president.

    Bibliography: p.
    Includes index.
    1. Presidents–United States–Election. I. Title.
JK528.B74   324.6'0973   81–43597
ISBN 0–8191–2287–4   AACR2
ISBN 0–8191–2288–2 (pbk.)

Contents

PREFACE

The entire process of selecting a president of the United States has been both spirited and colorful throughout the history of the Nation. The position, office and powers, is almost an American invention. The selection arrangement is such an invention. That uniqueness, long entrenced in our political ways, has frequently, indeed almost continuously, been the object of concern about its permanence and whether it fits the political tenor of the time.

The pages which follow are designed to present the issues surrounding the pattern for selecting the president, provide an update about them, and to offer a plan for altering the present system.

I have relied on the works of others and hope to have given them proper recognition and to have fairly and accurately reflected the views of those whose positions on the issues have been published.

I wish to express appreciation to the University of Nebraska Foundation for financial assistance from the Fund for Research on the U.S. Congress.

Some personal acknowledgements are in order. I am especially indebted to my colleague, Professor Susan Welch, for her advice and encouragement and for adjusting my class schedule to permit time for research and writing, and I am grateful to my former student, G. P. Machal, for helpful suggestions.

I have a better understanding of the role of congressional committees from discussions with former U.S. Senator for Nebraska, Roman L. Hruska, who served on the Senate Committee on the Judiciary and the Subcommittee on the Constitution.

Ramona Farmer provided expert typing of the final draft. My wife, Marion, helped with the proof, and I am thankful for her patience and understanding while this effort was in the making.

Lincoln, Nebraska Adam C. Breckenridge
         University of Nebraska-Lincoln

Chapter I.   Introduction

The decision in 1980 by John B. Anderson of Illinois to seek the presidency as an independent candidate following his unsuccessful attempt to gain the Republican nomination caused many observers to conclude that the electoral college would not elect a president that year.

The assumption was that Anderson would either win a plurality in some states, especially those with large urban populations and therefore their electoral votes, or would siphon off enough popular votes presumably which otherwise for the most part would have been cast for President Carter, and in either event, or both, neither Carter nor Ronald Reagan would receive the needed minimum of 270 electoral votes.

These forecasts were accompanied by criticisms of the entire presidential electoral system although directed primarily to the electoral college and were repeated periodically during the weeks of the summer and fall campaign period. They were noticeably highlighted by the major media, but also by publications not having a wide national popular circulation. Even the highly regarded Congressional Quarterly appeared to have been sympathetic to opponents of the electoral college. As early as May 1980, "CQ" carried a banner that the "Anderson Bid Highlights Electoral Pitfalls." And on the eve of the election its frontispiece for the issue of October 25 had the label "Will it Work in 1980?"

There was no long wait on election night to have the results. Indeed President Carter conceded the election to Reagan before the polls had closed in some western parts of the nation. Anderson received no electoral votes and Reagan won handily with 489 votes to 49 for Carter. (If Reagan had not carried all of the large states of Illinois (26), Ohio (25), Michigan (21), New Jersey (17), New York (41), and Pennsylvania (27) or even Texas (26), he would still have won the election with 306 votes).

Since opponents of the electoral college system consistently emphasize the possibility that the system could produce a minority president, that is one not also receiving a plurality of the total national popular vote, it may be noted that what was predicted by some in 1980 as a possible repeat of 1968 in closeness, Reagan received 43,899,248 total national popular votes, and 35,481,435 for Carter, with Anderson's total being 5,719,437. It was far from a repeat.

It was the 1968 campaign and electoral college and popular vote results, however, which produced the most recent and continuous effort, primarily in the U.S. Senate, to formally challenge the system for electing the president. Although much of the attention during the 1968 and 1980 campaigns centered on the third party "spoiler" candidates, Wallace and Anderson respectively, far broader criticisms were directed to the system which had operated since the first election of George Washington.

The three-way presidential race in 1968 prompted predictions that no candidate would receive a majority vote in the electoral college. Indeed, a "constitutional crisis" was forecast. Although the polls indicated that the two top contenders would be Richard M. Nixon and Hubert H. Humphrey, serious concerns were expressed that in order for either to win under the House of Representatives contingency plan (each state having one vote as determined by the state's House membership) some bargaining with George C. Wallace's supporters would be required for one of them to gain the majority needed. A prolonged delay or even a stalemate in the House was indicated by many.

In retrospect, of course, the gloomy predictions were only speculation. Some were faulty from the outset where based on the assumption that the House delegations in those states where Wallace won the electoral vote would all support him automatically or not engage in any bargaining of consequence. Although some of the newly elected House members in those states supported Wallace, not all did, and whether they did or not, it could not mean any mandate for his views. Furthermore, predictions of a "Constitutional Crisis" if the decision were made in the House overlooked the prospect that there could be some "faithless" electors who would cast their vote for Nixon or Humphrey and give one or the other the needed majority eliminating the need for any House consideration.

The electoral college, of course, produced a majority decision but with one defector who cast his vote for Wallace instead of Nixon, with Nixon winning

2

the presidency.

In that election Nixon received 301 electoral votes and a national total popular vote of 31,777,237. Humphrey's total was 191 electoral votes and 31,270,533. Wallace's strength was substantial. He had the support of 9,897,141 voters nationally and received 46 electoral votes.

Soon after the 91st Congress convened in January 1969, a number of resolutions were introduced in both houses for a variety of possible changes in the method of selecting the president. In the decade which followed, several were under active consideration, primarily by the Senate, to eliminate the electoral college with increasing focus on a plan for a direct national popular vote. Other plans gradually lost most of their supporters.

The record shows that the national popular vote proposal is highly controversial. Debate in and out of the Congress has been spirited. Congressional hearings have been extensive, especially in the Senate and the printed reports of these hearings are voluminous. During the last decade or so numerous articles and books have been published on the subject. Some present a strong defense of the electoral college system. Some denounce it and concentrate on its real or alleged shortcomings. Others are obvious in presenting a case for a national popular vote.

The purpose of this volume is to present the issues not only about the electoral college system, but also about related factors having bearing on any selection system. It cannot be assumed that the debate will concentrate wholly on a direct vote plan as the alternative. If a proposed Constitutional amendment does emerge from the Congress for consideration by the states, the decision to ratify or not will be based on a wide variety of facts, speculation, opinion, and ultimately judgments. Solid proof of positions taken will be difficult at best. The electoral college arrangement will have strong defenders. If a national popular vote plan is the one selected by the Congress, it, too, will have strong promoters. But if the amending process is to be fully aired, then the substantive issues should be clearly outlined. It is the purpose here to review the major proposals for change in the method of selecting the president as the best means of isolating these issues.

In addition to presenting the essentials of the several prevailing plans, some additional features will be included which have heretofore received minimal attention. These will be featured:

First, since numerous public hearings have been held especially since 1969 and the printed results make up thousands of pages of testimony, reports, and statements, special attention will be given to those hearings, with concentration on those conducted by the appropriate Senate subcommittee and the Senate Committee on the Judiciary. Attention will be given to the substantive nature of the hearings, the witnesses, their selection process, the degree of balance in the presentation of the issues, and the division of views by members of the subcommittee or committee. Unless the hearings are but a facade, what was said or included in the hearings must be considered as a significant feature of the amending process.

Second, little or no attention has been given to the Maine District Plan for the selection of presidential electors which has been in effect beginning with the 1972 election. An analysis of the Maine arrangement is given in Chapter V.

Third, the essentials of the Senate debate in 1979 on the national popular vote plan will be reviewed. An analysis of the vote in the Senate, rejecting the plan, will be made.

Fourth, since the Senate rejected the national vote proposal, an alternative arrangement is presented in Chapter X.

Fifth, to assist readers who wish to have additional materials to review, a Bibliographic Note is made as a part of the Appendix.

In the chapters which follow, these considerations will be addressed:

1) What are the major objections to the electoral college system?

2) What are the objectives to be achieved by any change?

3) What criteria are indicated?

4) What are the possible effects of a proposal on our established political institutions?

5) Is the "cure" likely to produce a "Constitutional Crisis" where none has yet occurred?

6) What uncertainties remain under the several proposals?

7) Since the Senate rejected the national vote plan in 1979, is there an alternative plan which might be acceptable?

Throughout the decade of the 1970s, consideration of proposals by the Senate Committee on the Judiciary reflected a reluctance, indeed strong opposition to undertake change by a series of amendments. It should be recalled that the provisions in the U.S. Constitution concerning the presidency have been subject to several amendments. If reference made only to those ratified since the adoption of the Bill of Rights, there have been six amendments and if the 14th amendment is included because of reference to presidential electors, then seven times. None of these affected the executive power of the president and for the most part were concerned with the selection process. Three additional amendments greatly enlarged the electorate but it is difficult to assess that impact on the presidency. In one way or another the amendments did alter the shape of our political institutions and abolishing the electoral college, for example, could be the most substantive change yet affecting the presidency and the federal system.

As the debate on this matter continues, individuals of wisdom and good judgment will arrive on opposing sides. Readers of this work will arrive opposing each other. Similarly, those in the Congress and the state legislatures will not have a high degree of unanimity in the decision-making process.

But, then, constitution-making is never a simple undertaking.

Chapter II. The Electoral College

The method of selecting the president of the
United States has been a subject of some controversy
from the beginning. On September 4, 1787, James
Wilson of Pennsylvania is recorded as having made this
comment in the Constitutional Convention about selecting the president:

> This subject has greatly divided the house, and
> will also divide people out of doors. It is in
> truth the most difficult of all on which we have
> had to decide.[1]

Now, nearly two hundred years later, it remains a
subject which frequently divides people "out of doors."
But as with other features of the U.S. Constitution,
the plan for selecting the president recognized the
federal nature for government, not a wholly national
one, a mix of centralized government, dual arrangements, nation and state, and assumptions for a large
measure of government remaining unspecified to be
left to the discretion of the states forming the Union.
Not only did the Constitution provide for a federal
arrangement for selecting a president it emphasized
the distinct role of the states in selecting members
of the Congress. Until the adoption of the 17th
Amendment in 1913 members of the Senate were selected
by the state legislatures and to this time state
equality is preserved by guaranteeing equal numbers
of Senators to each of them.

Several proposals for selecting the president
were presented to the Convention in 1787. These included election by both houses of the Congress or the
Senate only. One provided for direct popular election.
Another would have the election by an assembly of
governors of the several states or by electors chosen
by the governors. Still another would have authorized
election by electors chosen by the state legislatures
or by electors chosen by popular vote in state districts with the chosen electors meeting together to
choose the president. A modification of election by
the Congress would have given the decision to a body of
electors when a president sought to succeed himself in
office.

On two occasions the elections of the president by
the Congress was approved by the delegates, but this

was later rejected apparently in the belief that the president should be chosen independently of the legislative branch, thus giving greater footing to the concept of the separation of powers and a greater degree of independence between the legislative and executive branches.

Some of the delegates supported the plan for direct popular national election with expressions of support by James Madison, James Wilson, Gouverneur Morris, Hugh Williamson, John Dickinson, Elbridge Gerry, and Daniel Carroll. But objection to direct election was voiced by others because it was believed the people would not or could not be sufficiently well informed about the candidates and there would be a tendency for people to vote for the candidate from their own state or immediately surrounding states. There was concern also that the more populous states would generally dominate--a concern which has remained to this time.

The electoral college idea was advanced by James Wilson. His original plan called for electors to be chosen by state districts, but this was defeated. Alternative proposals included electors chosen by the state legislatures or by the Congress, but as with other earlier proposals these also were rejected. At this juncture a renewal for election of electors chosen by popular vote was also rejected.

The final form, endorsed by the delegates, was as follows:

Each state shall appoint, in such manner as the Legislature thereof may direct, a Number of Electors, equal to the whole Number of Senators and Representatives to which the State may be entitled in the Congress; but no Senator or Representative or Person holding an Office of Trust or Profit under the United States, shall appoint an Elector.

Obviously, this provision emphasized the federal principle, first with the equality granted each state with two electors based on Senate representation, and second with electors additionally chosen equal to the membership in the House. Specific authority was given to the state legislature to determine the method of choosing the electors. Thus, the arrangement clearly recognized the position of the states in the selection process. Although the decisions of the U.S. Supreme

Court have partially curtailed the independence of state authority in choosing members of the House in the reapportionment cases, the states are still empowered to arrange districts if the judicial guidelines are met. This has not affected the number of House seats for each state nor the number of electors.

The idea of a national assembly of electors was not included in the Constitution, rather the electors were directed to meet separately in each state to make their decision.

The Congress was given authority to determine the time of choosing the electors and the day for the state by state vote and required that the day be the same throughout the United States. Nearly a century ago the U.S. Supreme Court had occasion to deal with the status of electors. It said in part:

> The sole function of the presidential electors is to cast, certify and transmit the vote of the State for President and Vice President of the nation. Although the electors are appointed and act under and pursuant to the Constitution of the United States, they are no more officers or agents of the United States than are members of the State legislatures when acting as electors of federal senators, or the people of the States when acting as electors of representatives in Congress . . . . In accord with provisions of the Constitution, Congress has determined the time as of which the number of electors shall be ascertained, and the days on which they shall be appointed and shall meet and vote in the States, and on which their votes shall be counted in Congress; has provided for the filling by each State, in such manner as its legislature may prescribe, of vacancies in its college of electors; and has regulated the manner of certifying and transmitting their votes to the seat of the national government, and the course of proceeding in their opening and counting them.[2]

The Constitution is silent about the details for choosing the electors except that the legislature in each state is given apparent discretion. A uniform plan was not indicated and whether this was due to difficulty in finding agreement among the delegates or a reflection that this was a proper matter for individual state determination is uncertain. It does indicate further emphasis of the role of the states in the selection of a president.

Although not all of the delegates may have agreed with the views expressed by Alexander Hamilton in _Federalist_ 68, it was assumed that however selected, the electors would exercise their judgment in making a choice for president. There appears to have been no presumption of having instructions given them on their voting as electors. This independence has long since been generally abandoned, but not quite, and since that independence has remained it is one of the continuing issues about the electoral college. The independence of a few electors gave rise to the label of the "faithless" elector.

Hamilton wrote in _Federalist_ 68:

> The mode of appointment of the Chief Magistrate of the United States is almost the only part of the system, of any consequence, which has escaped without severe censure, or which has received the slightest mark of approbation from its opponents. The most plausible of these, who has appeared in print, has even deigned to admit that the election of the President is pretty well guarded.

> . . . the immediate election should be made by men most capable of analyzing the qualities adapted to the station, and acting under circumstances favorable to deliberation, and to a judicious combination of all the reasons and inducements which were proper to govern their choice. A small number of persons, selected by their fellow-citizens from the general mass, will be most likely to possess the information and discernment to such complicated investigations.

> It was also peculiarly desirable to afford as little opportunity as possible to tumult and disorder . . . The choice of _several_, to form an intermediate body of electors, will be much less apt to convulse the community with any extraordinary or violent movements, than the choice of _one_ who was himself to be the final object of public wishes.

The extent to which the separate sets of electors, state by state, practice deliberation and a "judicious combination of all the reasons and inducements which were proper to govern their choice" is not a matter of major concern here. The issue rather has been how to require the electors to reflect the popular vote in each state and thereby prevent an independent action by one or more electors.

In the early years the states experimented, appropriately, with several modes of "appointing" electors. These were summarized in an opinion of the U.S. Supreme Court in 1892:

> Therefore, on reference to contemporaneous and subsequent action under the clause, we should expect to find, as we do, that various modes of choosing the electors were pursued, as, by the legislature itself on joint ballot; by the legislature through a concurrent vote of the two houses; by vote of the people for a general ticket; by vote of the people in districts; by choice partly by the people voting in districts and partly by the legislature; by choice by the legislature from candidates voted for by people in districts; and in other ways, as, notably, by North Carolina in 1792, and Tennessee in 1796 and 1800. No question was raised as to the power of the State to appoint, in any mode its legislature saw fit to adopt, and one that a single method, applicable without exception, must be pursued in the absence of an amendment to the Constitution. The district system was largely considered the most equitable, and Madison wrote that it was that system which was contemplated by the framers of the Constitution, although it was soon seen that its adoption by some states might place them at a disadvantage by a division of their strength, and that a uniform rule was preferable.[3]

The reference to a "division of strength" meant that the candidate in a given state who had the majority or plurality of the popular vote might not carry all electoral districts.

Critics of the electoral college generally deny that the plan rests on any "federal" process and it is not a mix of national and state authority by two somewhat independent spheres of government. In a 1934 decision, the U.S. Supreme Court said that "while presidential electors are not officers or agents of the federal government, they exercise federal functions under, and discharge duties in virtue of authority con-

ferred by, the Constitution of the United States."[4]
Presumably, therefore, the process of election was
not originally resident in the states but is granted
only as a result of provisions in the Constitution.
Assuming that is a correct interpretation, there is
an obvious mix of national and state authority.
Similarly, there was no antecedent for the selection
of a president of the "whole" people or of the colonies
prior to the adoption of the Constitution.

The procedures for selecting the president and
vice president was destined for early difficulty.
Suffice to state, the ballots for the two offices in
the election of 1800 resulted in a tie vote and the
contingency arrangement wisely included was put into
operation. The result, however, was to require, by
the 12th Amendment, that the voting for the two offices be done separately and that problem has not arisen
since.

Several other amendments have been directed to
issues in the presidential selection process, albeit
some less apparent than others. The so-called Civil
War Amendments, the 13th, 14th, and 15th, affected the
process by broadening the electoral voting base.
Similarly, the extension of the suffrage to women by
the 19th Amendment and more recently the lowering of
the voting age to 18 through the 26th Amendment have
had an impact on voter decision-making which is yet
to be adequately assessed.

Although the total number of presidential electors
was more or less static in recent decades especially
by limiting the membership in the House to 435, the
admission of Hawaii and Alaska as states increased
the number of Senators by four and therefore the number of electors. Later, in 1961, with the adoption of
the 23rd Amendment, the District of Columbia was
granted the state minimum of three electoral votes
bringing the current total to 538.

Other Amendments to the Constitution have also
affected the presidential selection process. The 20th
Amendment shifted the contingency arrangement. If no
candidate was elected by the electoral college and the
responsibility thereby fell to the House, the membership elected in the presidential year would have the
assignment rather than the expiring "lame duck" House.
This change was in harmony with the date for commencing
the new term of office for the Congress and to give a
"fresh mandate" from the voters, albeit indirectly.

The 22nd Amendment denied the right of the electors from selecting an individual as president for more
than two full terms. What impact this restriction has
had on the presidency and the selection process is not
easily determined. It is interesting to note that
although a single term of office was explored in the
Convention of 1787, the four-year term without any
Constitutional restriction for succession was in effect
until after World War II when the 22nd Amendment was
made effective. Currently, there is a renewal of
interest in a single term of six years to eliminate the
burden of an incumbent seeking a second term and yet
one long enough to give a president time to pursue his
programs in and out of the Congress.

The 24th Amendment outlaws the use by the states
of taxes as a condition for voter eligibility in
balloting for members of the Congress or presidential
electors. This arose because of the use of the poll
tax in a few states to deny, in effect, otherwise
unencumbered voting privileges. Made effective in
1964, the Amendment was born in and adopted during a
period when the national mood was for uniformity and
conformity and minimum standards and the removal of
any state requirements which limited free voter participation.

A review of the operation of the electoral college
system requires some comment about the major criticisms and real or alleged shortcomings of the system.
Highlighting them is the "unit rule" wherein the
candidate having the highest vote, majority or plurality of popular votes, receives the entire electoral
vote of a state--if there are no faithless electors--
except in Maine which uses the District plan. This
winner-take-all arrangement will be considered later.

A close companion usually under scrutiny by
critics is the contingency plan if the election shifts
to the House.

Implicit in these two features is whether the
system is so undemocratic as to necessitate its abandonment and substitute a scheme such as the national
direct popular vote plan.

The relative absence of reliable data for elections in the early years makes it difficult to review
them in contrast to more recent time. The electoral
vote, of course, is available. Usually the historical
role of the electoral college begins with the election

of 1800, previously mentioned.

Six presidential elections later, in 1824, the contingency plan was used since the electoral college did not produce a presidential candidate with a majority of the vote. Hence, the decision was made in the House. Although Andrew Jackson received a reported 43.13% of the national popular vote and 37.93% of the electoral vote, his nearest opponent, John Quincy Adams, received 30.54% of the popular vote and 32.18% of the electoral vote. In the House vote, with one vote for each state, Adams was elected by a vote of thirteen to seven, with four votes going to William H. Crawford. The other major candidate was Henry Clay whose supporters shifted their vote to Adams.

Shortly thereafter in the election of 1836, the Senate was called upon to select the Vice-President as provided for in the 12th Amendment. In that election, Richard M. Johnson, Democratic running mate of Martin Van Buren received 147 of the 294 electoral votes, one short of the required majority. Twenty-three electors voted for Van Buren, but not for Johnson. The Democratic majority in the Senate chose Johnson. There have been no other Senate choices.

The next major test of the capacity of the electoral college system to produce a president was in 1860 when there were four candidates, three of whom were Democrats of varying styles, but Abraham Lincoln received the majority of the electoral vote and a reported slightly less than 40% of the total national popular vote. The contingency plan did not have to be used.

When the election results are not close in national total popular votes or in the electoral college vote, there has been little national interest in how the results came about. An exception was in 1876 and it is an election highlighted as presenting the most serious and flagrant shortcoming of the presidential selection system. In that election, Samuel J. Tilden, the Democratic candidate, had a majority of the national popular vote of 50.99% and about 250,000 votes over the Republican candidate, Rutherford B. Hayes. Ultimately Hayes was elected, but not under the process outlined in the Constitution. At issue were the electoral votes in four states. The decision for Hayes came from a recommendation of an especially constituted Congressional Electoral Commission which reportedly voted along partisan lines to approve

14

electoral votes in contest and grant Hayes one more
vote than Tilden. Criticism of this action and the
method used to arrive at it should be directed to
faulty processes in the states involved and the method
used to certify the electoral vote. Some of the
apparent confusion then shifted to the Congress and may
have resulted from the distresses coming from the
phasing out of the reconstruction time-table.

The 1888 election produced concerns among both
defenders and critics of the electoral college. Again,
the issue centered on the disparity between the total
national popular vote and the electoral college majority. Grover Cleveland received the highest national
popular vote of 48.66%, but only 42% of the electoral
vote. Benjamin Harrison had a popular vote of 47.86%
but an electoral vote of 58%. Harrison won the
election with a popular vote of about 100,000 less
than Cleveland. In most of the appraisals about the
electoral college system this election is also highlighted not alone because of the lower popular vote
for the winner but in arithmetic calculations afterward
of how Cleveland could have won with a few thousand
votes cast differently here and there. New York state
is usually cited where had that been the case, Cleveland would have won the presidency.

The experience of the electoral college arrangement shows challenges to the principle of majority
rule. At issue is the degree of disparity or distortion between the electoral college vote and the total
national popular vote. Minor differences appear not to
disturb the value of the present system. In the
election of 1860, considered above, it should be
recalled that Lincoln's name did not appear on the
ballot in several states. Stephen A. Douglas received
29 percent of the popular vote, but only 4 percent of
the electoral vote. Much later, in the election of
1912, Woodrow Wilson received 42 percent of the popular
vote with his electoral vote reaching 82 percent. More
than three decades later in 1936, Alfred M. Landon
gained about 37 percent of the popular vote, but only 2
percent of the electoral vote--translated into eight
electoral votes. Franklin D. Roosevelt, in contrast,
received nearly 60 percent of the popular vote and 98
percent of the electoral vote.

Brief reference has been made to the unit rule in
the allocation of electoral votes. It has both critics
and strong defenders. And as noted it is used in all
states except in Maine. Critics argue that under this

rule·votes for the losing candidate do not count. As early as 1824 Senator Thomas Hart Benton of Missouri is reported as having observed in the Senate: "To lose their votes is the fate of all minorities, and it is their duty to submit; but this (the electoral college) is not the case of votes lost, but of votes taken away, added to those of the majority and given to a person to whom the minority is opposed."[5] It is not a very solid argument for if there is a loser there is also a winner. If the electoral college vote is ignored, the 1932 election can be cited where nearly sixteen million popular votes were cast for Herbert C. Hoover, all votes for a loser.

Different circumstances prevailed in the 1844 election and did not produce a noticeable disparity between the national popular vote and the electoral vote. The results show, however, that had New York voters voted differently and shifted about 3,000 votes, the election would have gone to Henry Clay. Small voter shifts in the election of 1884 would have produced a President James G. Blaine.

The real or alleged blemishes in the electoral college system serve to demonstrate how it has performed when under some stress. There have not been many such occasions. But these arose and had they not, the major recent criticisms would now likely be reduced to whether the system is sufficiently democratic.

It is apparent that the framers of the Constitution wanted some system of majority rule. Having rejected the national popular vote proposals, declared for a federal design with a strong position for the states, the framers also recognized that the system might not always work as intended. Thus, the need for the inclusion of a contingency plan. This was fundamental since even with only two candidates neither might receive a majority of the electoral vote. With more than two, the prospects were far greater that a majority vote might not be realized.

The electoral college process rests on an arrangement of multiples of state pluralities or majorities, but if they do not produce a majority, then some insurance was needed to insure the election. That is the purpose of the contingency plan. Its essentials are:

The person having the greatest number of votes (electoral) for President, shall be the

16

President, if such number be a majority of the whole number of electors appointed; and if no person have such majority, then from the persons having the highest numbers not exceeding three on the list of those voted for as President, the House of Representatives shall choose immediately, by ballot, the President. But in choosing the President, the votes shall be taken by States, the representation from each State having one vote; a quorum for this purpose shall consist of a member or members from two-thirds of the States, and a majority of all the States shall be necessary to make a choice.

An analysis of the claimed undemocratic features of the contingency plan will be included in challenges to the entire electoral process in the next chapter.

FOOTNOTES

1. *Documents Illustrative of the Formation of the Union of the American States*, 69th Cong., 1st sess., House Document No. 398 (1927), p. 664.

2. *In re Green*, 134 U. S. 377, 379-380 (1890).

3. *McPherson* v. *Blacker*, 146 U. S. 1, 28-29 (1892).

4. *Burroughs and Cannon* v. *U. S.*, 290 U. S. 534, 545 (1934).

5. *Annals of Congress*, v. 41, p. 170 (1824).

Chapter III. Challenges to the Electoral College System

This chapter is designed to place focus upon the major issues and challenges to the system of electing the president. Some references to them have been made earlier in association with the system in operation.

It is an election system which must be considered, not one or more of its procedures in isolation from the whole of it. It is comparatively easy to pinpoint some of the system's characteristics for praise or scorn, but pitfalls may result from that kind of an excursion.

The long-standing Constitutional arrangement for the ultimate selection of a president has always produced one and on schedule, albeit with a few skirmishes en route. Of all the objections to the arrangement the capstone of criticisms contain an element of "scare" tactics, that is, if the electoral college does not produce a majority, then a constitutional "crisis" results, since a decision in the House is so outmoded and archaic that the general public would not accept confidence in the results. If it did, then unless the decision was in favor of the candidate with the highest total national popular vote, the "crisis" would be no less severe.

Assuming a dictionary definition of "crisis" is sufficient here, it means that it is a turning point which is crucial or decisive and a situation whose outcome decides whether possible bad consequences will follow. To date, predictions of a crisis have not been accurate.

A possible crisis is only one of the challenges to the system. Other criticisms are that the system is so filled with defects that it must be scrapped. The briefs which now follow are to show what these are claimed to be and to parenthetically indicate some response to assist in placing the objection in perspective.

Election to a popular vote loser.

A candidate might receive the required majority of the electoral vote, but not a corresponding majority or plurality of the total national popular vote. Would a president elected under these conditions be able to govern effectively? Would the "people" consider the new president had a mandate from the electorate? Or, would he or she be considered automatically ineffective and thereby impair the presidency throughout the term? Would the president, elected under these circumstances, have enough support from the general public to permit or provide the leadership necessary in the executive branch, and if so, would they be adverse in the working relationships with the Congress? (As will be noted elsewhere, the tie-in between the electoral college vote, a majority, and the total national popular vote, at least a plurality, is the cornerstone of the views of the most majoritarian who holds that unless the national plebiscite supports the winner in the electoral college then the system is basically defective).

House contingency plan.

If no candidate received a majority of the electoral vote the decision would go to the House as provided in the Constitution, the 12th Amendment, with a selection to be made from the top three of the voting in the electoral college, not national popular votes, and each state would have one vote to cast. To arrive at the vote, the delegation of a state determines how it will be cast. It is alleged that if a state's delegation is evenly divided particularly along party lines, then the state involved and its people would be disenfranchised. That could happen and the state could not cast a vote. In the recent debates about the electoral college in the Senate and in discussions in the hearings of the 1970s it was frequently stated that had the 1968 election been decided in the House it would have been done after bargaining and "wheeling and dealing" with a major adverse impact on principles. This criticism was directed toward the influence George Wallace's supporters might have brought to bear on the decision.

But even if bargaining was not involved, the critics insist that the House contingency feature is undemocratic since each state is given equal weight in having a single vote. Differences in population among the states are substantial, of course, with the result that the lone member of the House from North Dakota would be equal to the New York delegation of thirty-four. (If the electoral college is to continue in some form, some contingency feature seems imperative. Alternatives to the existing House plan will be considered later).

Millions of votes don't count.

The present plan provides, even guarantees, (that countless voters are in effect disenfranchised or that their vote is not actually reflected in the electoral college count.) This criticism refers, generally, to the winner-take-all or unit rule in allocating votes in a state. Maine, of course, is the exception with the District plan. The basic argument against the unit rule is that the minority of the voters are having their votes "taken away" and "given" to another candidate, the one with the majority or plurality of the state's popular vote. It is further claimed that it is fallacious to state that losers lose nothing since the final tally shows the winner with all the electoral votes and the loser with none. (One response to this observation is to institute some form of proportional allocation of votes. This is generally in harmony with one of the proposals of long standing to retain the electoral college vote feature but distribute the votes in proportion to the popular vote cast to each candidate. The essentials of this plan will be given in Chapter V).

Threat to the two-party tradition.

The electoral college system threatens the fundamental advantages of the traditional two-party system since it encourages third parties and makes it even more difficult to obtain a majority decision. The 1968 election is usually cited. It was thought by some that the 1980 election would be placed along side as a companion, but this did not come to pass. It is also claimed that the present arrangement discouraged even healthy two-party competition where one-party strength is substantial and many voters really have no choice. Does he vote for his choice knowing or believing his candidate cannot win? The loser gets no electoral votes and this may even encourage a stronger one-party state. (As will be noted later, this debate is often spirited in considering the effects of a direct popular election arrangement and whether it would strengthen or weaken the two-party tradition. Recent elections do not show strong evidence that many one-party states remain. Indeed, the only true one-party area in the elections of 1972, 1976 and 1980 was the District of Columbia. The voters there have consistently supported the Democratic candidate and with substantial majorities).

<u>Blocs of voters decide elections</u>.

The past and prospective power of bloc-voting has generally rested on campaign appeals to particular population groups in various regions and in post election analysis. Assuming the stance of proponents of two-party domination as essential but also oppose the electoral college system, it is alleged that a state-by-state decision in determining the final electoral count automatically gives especially identifiable groups of voters a built-in advantage and usually identified are ethnic or minority elements of the population. This is based on the belief that such groups usually vote in a uniform way and even for the same party candidate election after election. Where this prevails other candidates are discouraged from making any but a feeble effort to win support for to do so would be an exercise in futility. In a close election, critics of the electoral college system insist, bloc voting will determine the direction of all the state's electoral votes, again shutting out a great proportion of the total voter decision, thus distorting the result. (There are many evidences that bloc voting does exist whether by ethnic groups or otherwise. Curiously, the arguments about bloc voting directed at the electoral college system are used by opponents of the plan for a direct national popular vote who at the same time support the electoral college arrangement).

<u>Shifts of a few votes can change the outcome</u>.

Re-doing the election on Wednesday mornings following a presidential election has long been a favorite exercise for many. Often it occurs during election night. Central to this activity is the showing that in a close race in the electoral college vote count a shift here and there of a few hundred or a few thousand popular votes would change the outcome. This numbers game is used by critics of the electoral college system who insist that if there had been these small alterations in what the voters actually did there could be even greater distorions between the popular vote tally and the electoral vote. They indicate strongly that under the popular vote plan the decision would be clear-cut. (Second guessing voters is risky business. Furthermore, if the national popular vote plan was in effect a shift of popular votes would have produced different results. In 1888 about 100,000 were involved. In 1968 some 500,000 would have been needed, but there were more than seventy million votes cast!).

The "faithless elector".

That the framers of the Constitution assumed that the electors could make independent judgments in casting their vote in no way endears the continuation of the <u>person</u> of the elector to their critics. For a long time it has been assumed that the electoral vote will or should reflect precisely the plurality or majority state popular vote. The record shows, of course that departures have occurred. As recently as the 1976 election the vote of a Washington elector was cast for Ronald Reagan instead of Ford who had the majority of the popular vote. Depending on how the tabulations are made there are eight other occasions on which electors chose an independent route. To prevent this some states have enacted statutes requiring that the electors vote to reflect the popular vote. The problem has been to fix a satisfactory method of enforcement. The Congress determines whether to accept the votes as tabulated and certified from each state and this has almost always been done. There is one notable exception when in 1872 Horace Greeley had died after the general election and the electoral votes cast for him were not accepted. (There appears to be general agreement even among adherents to the electoral college that the person of the elector should be done away with and substitute the automatic plan. This plan will be considered later).

The presidency is a national office.

Electoral college critics have long insisted as have countless students of the presidency that the office is a truly <u>national</u> one and always has been. As such, the electoral college vote should not in any way be one other than to reflect the national popular vote. The view that the office is a <u>federal</u> one has few supporters. Indeed, the presidency is generally viewed as being the only national officer election nationally and as the single executive it could not be considered in any other way. This strikes a hard blow to the position that the election of the president even if a national officer is done under a federal process. If there is any doubt, therefore, eliminating the electoral college would clear up the matter for all time. (Although the reapportionment rulings have cleared up many concerns about the democratic nature of elections for members of the House, critics of any <u>federal</u> presidency have not found much strength in opposing the equality feature for the Senate).

"One-man, one-vote."

Although sidestepping the issue about state
equality in the Senate, critics of the electoral
college insist that the electoral college vote is
calculated to violate the one-man, one-vote requirement. Arithmetic calculations abound to show the
disparity of guaranteed equality of voter strength, for
example, between New York or California and Nevada or
Alaska. These latter states have the minimum of three
electoral votes each notwithstanding the substantial
population difference with the former. The two votes
based on the Senate should be eliminated even if the
electoral college arrangement is continued. (The
critics may be confusing their issues. Voting, per se,
is primarily a matter of state concern even with some
heavy doses of U. S. surveillance. Voters may vote if
they wish and for whom they wish and their votes are
counted as equal--barring some human or mechanical
error or fraud in the counting process. This should be
the fundamental meaning of "one-man, one-vote." But it
has been extended, erroneously, to challenges to the
electoral college. The one-man, one-vote judicial
pronouncement came from the reapportionment cases
involving the allocation of seats in the House or the
state legislatures. These issues were not about the
equality of the vote but about inequalities in ratios
of numbers of the population in a district. Numbers
of people in an area may bear little similarity to the
number of voters in that same area or even the number
eligible to vote when compared to another adjacent
area).

A president of one party, a vice-president of
another.

The 12th Amendment requires a separate ballot for
each of these positions and theoretically the electors
could vote for one of one party and one from another.
This danger should be prevented, state the critics.
Even though the vice-president is given little authority by the Constitution, presidents have authorized
some of them to perform some important functions.
Challengers to the possibility that the two might be
from different parties indicate that it would be
politically unacceptable for this practice to prevail.
Furthermore, matters would be intensified should a
vice-president of a different party succeed to the
presidency due to the death, resignation or disability

24

of the president. It is claimed that such a shift in the office would have damaging consequences. (The prospects of having the two offices filled by individuals of different political party affiliations is highly remote and could be prevented by use of the automatic plan for the casting of electoral votes. - What critics often overlook is that presidents and their vice-presidents are often at odds in policy matters and political ideology and a party label difference might not be as great as alleged. It should be noted that the same criticism is made about the use of the House and Senate contingency plans for the election of the president and vice-president).

Disparity in voter qualifications.

State constitutions have long provided for voter qualifications. In addition state legislatures have been authorized to detail the process or even provide for additional standards. The result has been for them to have enacted a variety of voter requirements lacking in national uniformity or consistency. These have included residency periods of varying lengths, age minima, the style or type of ballots, including the use or prohibition of the use of voting machines, registration procedures, hours for voting, the general administration of voting, requirements for the counting of ballots, methods of handling appeals, and the former provisions in a few for poll taxes, literacy tests, and restrictions because of sex or national origin. All now require that a voter be a citizen of the U.S.

Generally, any person eligible to vote for the candidates for the most numberous branch of the state legislature could vote for presidential electors. And this now appears to be universal in the Nation. Restrictions have been pared down either by national mandate or state initiated action. But many variations among the states remain and may adversely affect the national quality of the participation of voters regardless of residence. Challengers apparently wish to provide a nationally prescribed uniform residency period, uniform registration procedures including same day registration, uniform balloting regulations, rules concerning the speed and method of vote-counting, controls over the release of the results, and a likely shift to the U. S. courts for all challenges to voting and votes. (These different features do not represent an exhaustive list. They are presented to indicate the way by which opponents of the electoral college arrangement associate variables among the

states and nationalization of the election system.
If the electoral college system were done away,
presumably the Congress would standardize all election
operations. Some suggestions include the extension of
the franchise nationally to legal resident aliens. If
this activity were accomplished by national enactment,
the states and local subdivisions would be virtually
forced to accede to similar arrangements for state and
local elections).

The possibility of fraud.

On the whole, challenges to voting operations,
including making final decisions on the results are
matters of state concern. With over 170,000 voting
precincts nation-wide, the prospects for error, fraud-
ulent or not, are most likely. Critics of the
electoral college system argue that the prospects of
an improper count, including fraud, are far more likely
under prevailing arrangements than would be possible
under nationally prescribed ones. This may be a
matter of debate. It is claimed that leaving these
matters to the states, especially in close contests,
could extend knowing the final decision for weeks or
months and the new president might not be chosen on
schedule. The way to avoid that possibility is to
make procedures uniform, especially for judicial
review even remove state participation from such
review. (Undoubtedly the variables in standards and
procedures and interpretations of them produce
different results than would obtain under some national
uniform system. Some election officials may fail to
fulfill their obligations to insure a fair, accurate
voting. Some jurisdictions may be so ridden with
partisanship that the announced vote may be a farce.
But to assume that nationalizing the procedures would
automatically end such possibilities is faulty. Some
corrective matters could come about under the present
arrangement. The Electoral Count Act of 1887 could be
updated, for example. The states could be urged to
review and update all statutes involving election
administration).

Electoral college not understood by the voters.

It is charged that the electoral college not only
is a misnomer it is also a complex system not understood by the voter, that he could not explain it,
could not justify it. The criticism extends to college
graduates perhaps including some political science
majors! The argument extends beyond the smooth

workings of the "college" especially when the "understanding" includes the contingency plan if the electoral college did not produce a winner. A more simple system such as the direct national popular vote would very likely be more easily understood and explained. (But the electoral college system is not new, untried, or one with a history of failures. To suggest that the average voter believes that the president is elected as a result of the national popular vote is to deny the emphasis given in television tabulations, state by state, of the electoral vote, and viewed on election night by millions of those voters).

Large states dominate candidacy.

It is claimed that the more populous states, especially with the largest metropolitan areas, tend to dominate the nominating process under the present selection system, not only because of delegate strength in the conventions but also because the electoral vote is higher for any one of them than for an aggregate of small states. This influences the delegates to pick candidates from the larger states. The assumption is also that individuals from those states are likely to be better known nationally and can more readily gain support from large blocs of voters. This claimed advantage is said to be a ready-made edge in a presidential race and is an automatic disadvantage to candidates from the states with smaller populations.

(This argument has been worn thin by recent experience and in the exposure to possible candidates through the presidential primaries, the use of television, and earlier efforts by some to gain national recognition. It is also a less viable argument against the electoral college system since recent major party presidential candidates have been from not-so-large states as Arizona, Georgia, Maine, Missouri, and South Dakota).

Some of these challenges to the electoral college system are relatively minor. Some are not. But prior to any review of plans to alter the system it is essential that criteria for change be presented. What are the basic ingredients for a "better" method of electing the president? What guidelines should be developed and pursued?

The next chapter sets out some of the criteria which have been given recognition in recent years.

Chapter IV.   Criteria for Change

Presenting some ingredients for altering the
electoral college system through some guidelines or
criteria by which proposals may be examined and tested
is not an excursion into the unknown.   Others have
developed what each has considered to be the essentials for a better system.   Some of these appear to
have been developed from proposals for change rather
than having their origins in basic concepts of the
office of president and the relationships that office
has not only to the electorate, but to our total system
of political institutions and the framework for government in the United States.

It is not intended here to judge whether this or
that criterion was born of an emerging plan or whether
from philosophical reflection.   Rather the criteria
which have been developed need to be in view to permit
judgments to be made.   Basic to them is: what is
wanted?   What is sought?

In his testimony before the Subcommittee on the
Constitution of the Senate Committee on the Judiciary
on Friday July 22, 1977, Professor Herbert J. Storing
of the University of Virginia addressed the question
of the intent of the framers of the Constitution and
the ends they sought in the provision ultimately adopted for electing the president.   He summarized the
"ends of the system" in this way:[1]

First, it should provide for significant
participation by the people at large.
Second, it should foster political stability and
avoid the excesses of partisanship and factionalism that tend to form around important elections.
Third, it should give some special place of
influence to some individuals who are especially
informed of, and committed to, the process of
government.
Fourth, it should recognize that this is a Nation
of States and should give some weight to the
interests of States as such.
Fifth, it should leave the President independent
of any other institution of government, so far as
his election is concerned.
Sixth, it should, of course, tend to produce

Presidents of respectable character and intelligence.

In presenting these guidelines as the framers intent, Professor Storing defended the present system.

The present constitutional system for electing the President can be explained and popularly understood for what it is: a method of election that secures rather well the variety of benefits that the American Government is designed to secure--federalism, social diversity, governmental competence, stability, and fairness to individuals and to minorities.

In their "The Politics of Electoral College Reform," Lawrence D. Longley and Alan G. Braun identified three broad goals to be used in evaluating various plans for electoral college change.[2]

1. It should contribute to democracy, specifically--
   a. provide a basic equality of votes, and
   b. insure that the winning candidate is the one who received the most votes.

2. It should ensure the effectiveness of the presidency, specifically--
   a. contribute to its legitimacy through providing a broad mandate,
   b. provide a clear, easily comprehended, and distinctive source for the president's mandate,
   c. ensure a quick and decisive verdict not subject to conflicting claims, and
   d. avoid a constitutional crisis that might arise either through an extended election deadlock or through questionable proceedings and deals in the course of a contingent procedure.

3. It should both preserve and invigorate the political system, specifically--
   a. maintain the existing two-party system and encourage effective two-party competition while recognizing the legitimate right of potential third and fourth parties to electoral influence,
   b. encourage popular political participation--especially voter turnout--while minimizing campaign expenditures,

c. preserve federalism while securing an
equitable electoral influence for all
sections of the country in terms of
campaign time and political attention,
d. provide no systematic and inherent political biases favoring or hurting partisan,
ideological, or categoric groups in
American society, and
e. avoid any incentive for electoral fraud
and minimize the consequences of acciden-
tal electoral circumstances.

Longley and Braun then examined the several major
plans for change and gave an assessment as to which of
them met the criteria or met them in their judgment.
The result of that appraisal is readily observed from
the chapter heading of the evaluation: "Assessment:
The case for the Direct Vote Plan."

Some years earlier a 1969 Brookings Institution
report presented what it called "An Ideal Presidential
Election System." That system included four criteria.[3]

First, the election procedure should guarantee, insofar as possible, a quick election
decision with a clear-cut winner. The possibility
of a period of "constitutional crisis," during
which the identity of the victor is uncertain,
should be eliminated or at least minimized.

Second, the system should be democratic.
"The people's choice," the man with the most popular votes, should win.

Third, the President should be "legitimate,"
as defined by twentieth-century conceptions of
democracy in the United States. He should have a
margin of votes sufficient to be generally considered a "popular mandate to govern." Precise
parameters of legitimacy have never been established. An acceptable mandate is a margin of
victory somewhere between a plurality of one vote
and a majority of one vote.

Finally, the system should not undermine
accepted norms of American politics, particularly
the two-party system.

In his "Direct Election of the President,"
published in 1973, Professor Harvey Zeidenstein of
Illinois State University, and an avowed proponent of

direct election, seems to have endorsed the criteria of the Brookings report although he quarrels with the redundacy of some of it. He concludes with this observation: "If, as is our hope, a consensus can be reached on the four criteria, as defined, as the goals of a presidential election system, and if we have succeeded in removing disputations over the best means of achieving these goals, it but remains to explicitly recommend that means. It is direct popular election of the President by majority vote, with a popular runoff contingency if a majority is not reached on the first ballot."[4]

Zeidenstein also reviewed the criteria presented by proponents of the direct election plan before the Senate Committee on the Judiciary in 1970, but considered they were "self-serving" and clearly "intended to make direct election the only, inevitable means for reaching them." The three criteria in question were: guarantee that the man with the most votes is elected; count each vote equally; and provide the people themselves with the right to make the choice. He further observed that these criteria were too limited in that they "do not encompass at least two other values which legitimately may be required in an electoral system: a quick decision about who the winner is, and at least benign neutrality toward, and preferably outright support for, the two-party system."[5]

In his "The President: Basic Change Aborted: The Failure to Secure Direct Popular Election of the President, 1969-70," Professor Alan P. Sindler, University of California, Berkeley, analyzed several criteria.[6] He noted at the outset of his commentary that "the quarrel over electoral reform turned on the disputants' use of different criteria or of shared criteria weighted differently. Disagreement derived from the instability of any one election device to satisfy uniformly all criteria, some of which are competitive."

Some of the dispute about which among them is paramount or even applicable may stem from a desire by advocates of a particular proposal to have it meet the criteria. Sindler's review is warranted here.[7]

"The winning candidate should have the most popular votes."

Basic to this requirement is the standard one that "public acceptance" and the "election's legitimacy" would be in jeopardy without that result. He puts even greater emphasis on this criterion and places a stamp of the highest single standard of "commandment" and, indeed, the "first" of commandments. Furthermore, he states that "if the popular-vote decision has been frequently overturned in all categories of elections, including lopsided contests, the election method should be promptly disapproved." He does give recognition, however, to the argument by Professor Alexander Bickel that ". . . only an immensely dogmatic majoritarianism would insist that the so-called winner has the sole legitimate claim to office." This was in reference to presidential elections closely divided in popular vote.

"The winning candidate should have a minimum level of vote support."

The first of Sindler's criteria presumes a winner with a plurality of the total national popular vote. This second criterion is a modification of the first suggesting a requirement that there be no fewer than a certain percentage of that vote to provide a winner. His suggestions are no less than 35 percent in a three-way race or 30 percent in a four-way-race. If those circumstances prevailed, then a system for runoff between the two top contenders should be provided.

"Protecting and promoting two-partyism."

Sindler observes that most Senate spokesmen on this subject readily indicate their support to the two-party tradition. There is some evidence that even with that indication of support there is belief that any system should not automatically prevent third-party movements. Some others, especially those defending the electoral college, would make some modifications in the electoral college system if it did not mean diminishing the claimed tie between the two-party tradition and the electoral college.

"Maintaining checks and balances."

This criterion seems to center upon maintaining "presidential" government in the United States and even to enhance the independence of the presidency, especially if direct national popular election were provided. Sindler's analysis on this point includes a resume about the shift in positions by liberal blocs-- for the most of them--away from the present plan to direct election. It is this apparent shift, partly in the belief of political acceptance nationally, which has produced alleged liberal-conservative divisions in considering direct election proposals and the retention of the electoral college or some modification of the letter.

"Reflecting federalism?"

No clear-cut or definitive position can be made on this feature. Sindler notes that at the root of the difference about the place of "federalism" and its importance in the presidential selection system, is that we have a "national" president and not a "federal" one. Opponents of the electoral college would settle the matter for all time by eliminating it in favor of--preferably--direct national popular election. As Neal Peirce put it in his testimony before the Senate Committee on the Judiciary in 1977, "it seems to me that anyone who believes in the autonomy and responsibility of States in American Federalism--and I certainly do--should see that interposing a State between the people and choosing their President is a very strange way to protect either States or Federalism or any other recognizable value of representative government."[8]

As will be observed later, the impact of change in the system of electing the president on the American federal system is a continuing issue.

Sindler's last criterion is "Political feasibility." He was writing after the overwhelming favorable vote in the House of Representatives in 1969 for a Constitutional amendment which would scrap the electoral college system and substitute a scheme for direct national popular vote. (The Senate did not vote on the proposal at the time). It is Sindler's conclusion that the political acceptance of this plan not only in the House but in the results of polls among many state legislators made it the front runner.[9] At the time then President Nixon supported it, however reluctantly, presumably only if other plans failed to emerge through the Congress.

The above represent most of the guidelines or criteria which have come along in recent years pressing for electoral reform. From them there may be developed consensus and thereby wide-spread support for some modifications in the presidential selection system.

The next chapter is a review of the traditional

plans for change and includes some of the more rece
advanced proposals.

Congress, Senate, Judiciary Committee, ...nittee on the Constitution, Hearings on the Electoral College and Direct Election, 95th Cong., 1st sess., July 20, 22, 28, and August 2, 1977, p. 131.

2. Langley, Lawrence D., and Alan G. Braun, The Politics of Electoral College Reform. (New Haven: Yale University Press, 1975), pp. 75-76.

3. Included in the Appendix to Sayre, Wallace S., and Judith H. Parris, Voting for President: The Electoral College and the American Political System. (Washington, D. C.: The Brookings Institution, 1970), p. 153.

4. Zeidenstein, Harvey, Direct Election of the President. (Lexington, Mass.: Lexington Books, D. C. Heath and Company, 1973), p. 112.

5. Ibid., p. 106.

6. Sindler, Allan p., Policy and Politics in America, Case Study Two, (Boston: Little Brown and Company, 1973), p. 38.

7. Ibid., pp. 38-43.

8. U. S. Congress, Senate, Judiciary Committee, Hearings on the Electoral College and Direct Election, 95th Cong., 1st sess., January 27, February 1, 2, 7, and 10, 1977, p. 248.

9. Op. cit., pp. 44-45

Chapter V. Alternatives to the Electoral College: Proposals for Change

Proposals to change the Constitutional arrangement for the election of the president have been introduced into the Congress frequently almost from the beginning. The procedural problems arising from the election of 1800 produced the corrective 12th Amendment, but none of the substantive plans presented thereafter have emerged to be transmitted to the states for possible ratification. To critics of the electoral college system this has been both surprising and frustrating. To those who view the present system less severely, it is but testimony to its continued effectiveness. Under it, and for all elections, a president has been chosen and has taken office on schedule.

It seems unlikely, however, that even with this history of success, that critics of the "college" will be content to accept it for the indefinite future. Even staunch defenders of the system recognize some defects in it and probably would generally and readily agree to selective corrective measures, short, however, of abandoning its fundamentals.

The purpose of this chapter and the one following is to present the main features of several proposals which have been given varying degrees of support in and out of the Congress over the years. First, the automatic plan, then the proportional, some hybrid plans, and the district plan. The direct national popular vote plan will be treated in the latter chapter primarily because of the long standing effort in the Senate Committee on the Judiciary during the 1970s to gain congressional approval. Noted earlier was the formal acceptance of the direct vote plan in the House in 1969 and also its defeat in the Senate ten years later. These actions will be reflected in considering the hearings and debates.

The plan of presentation of the alternatives to the electoral college system is to state their essentials and then analyze the arguments which have been made both pro and con. It is believed that the reader can thereby determine whether one or the other of the plans is the most satisfactory if change is to be made or whether some other proposal or combination of them would fit criteria applied.

The Automatic plan.

The essential ingredient of the automatic plan for the election of the president is to abolish the person of elector. As the name of the plan indicates, (the electoral votes allocated to each state would be cast for the candidate receiving the highest popular vote in each state and determination of the winning candidate would follow in the same fashion as in the past.) In some proposals for an automatic plan other changes in the present system are included, particularly to alter the contingency feature in the event no candidate received the required majority of all electoral votes. Otherwise, (the primary purpose of the automatic plan is to eliminate the "faithless" elector,) those individuals who might decide, as some have done over the years, to cast their votes other than for the plurality or majority winner in his or her state.

Because of the history of having some faithless electors, some states have stipulated that any person serving as an elector must, as a condition of assuming that office, agree to observe the dictates of the voters. The problem is to ensure compliance. A state certifying officer must submit the votes of a state's electoral college members as they are cast. With the exception of instances involving disputed sets of electors, apparently the Congress has accepted these transmissions except in 1872 as observed earlier.

One presidential elector, acting independently, in 1968 cast his vote in North Carolina for George Wallace even though the plurality popular vote was in favor of Nixon. He was Dr. Lloyd W. Bailey, a medical doctor, and a Republican elector. Attention is given to his vote here, not that it altered the outcome of the election, but because of his testimony before the Senate Subcommittee on Constitutional Amendments of the Committee on the Judiciary in 1969. In that testimony he outlined his views about the place of the presidential elector and why he cast his vote as he did.[1]

> I think the elector should be free, abso-
> lutely free, from the time they are elected. This
> puts upon them a burden. A man who is elected
> under that circumstance will realize it. He is
> not automatic. It is not taken lightly. It is a
> serious job for a man to have that duty to cast
> the vote for the President of the United States.

If he is worth his salt he will look into these matters and do it in a very thorough way by backing up the position he takes. I think under that system we will have elections which are carried out by informed people.

Whether Dr. Bailey had long held these views may be questioned from some of his other testimony.

There was no pledge and there was no commitment made to any candidate. In the ensuing campaign I preferred Senator Thurmond or Governor Reagan to President Nixon. After the national conventions were held, I supported Governor Wallace, and I voted for him in the general election. I, along with many, was surprised that the Republican Party won in North Carolina. As an example of how lightly the position of Republican elector was taken, I had even forgotten that I was the elector until I was reminded by Dr. Stroud, the Second District Republican chairman, shortly before the general election. I did not think much more about being an elector until President Nixon began making appointments 2 weeks or so before the scheduled meeting of the electoral college. The names of men whose records I am familiar with began appearing in the news as appointees to high advisory positions for the executive branch of our Government; that forced me to realize that we are not going to get the changes in policy which we need and the electorate has so clearly shown that it wants . . . Another fact which could not be ignored was the overwhelming victory by Governor Wallace in my congressional district . . . This left no doubt about the wishes of the people in the district. Should they have been denied under a representative system of government?

North Carolina does not use the district plan in the selection of electors, rather follows the at-large or unit plan. Dr. Bailey would appear to like the district plan, but whether he did or not, his commentary amply illustrated the arguments in favor of the automatic plan for the electoral college voting apparatus. In a related sense, the Bailey vote meant that Nixon was deprived of one electoral vote which he would have received under the automatic plan.

Although the House contingency plan is not necessarily in contest in considering the automatic plan,

Dr. Bailey gave this view about voting for Wallace if the decision was shifted to the House.

> Senator Thurmond. Although you wouldn't have voted for Mr. Wallace if there had been danger of it going to the House because Mr. Humphrey might have been elected?

> Dr. Bailey. That is right.

Some other examples of faithless electors in recent years include a Tennessee elector in 1948 who voted for Strom Thurmond although Harry S. Truman carried the popular vote in that state. Eight years later, in 1956, Adlai E. Stevenson carried the state of Alabama, but one elector cast his vote for one Judge Walter E. Jones. And in 1960, an Oklahoma elector voted for Harry F. Byrd even though Nixon had carried the state. The most recent defector was in 1976 when an elector in the State of Washington voted for Reagan instead of the popular vote winner, Gerald R. Ford.

From these situations, it is evident that to date, at least, the major evil of the person of elector is voting contrary to the popular will. The act of voting as an elector is the only duty of the office and having cast that vote the functions of the office end. The value of the automatic plan is apparent, its supporters claim, although there may be some justification in retaining the person of elector. Some examples may be cited.

Brief mention has been made about the 1872 election when the Democratic candidate for president was Horace Greeley. He won the popular vote in six states. But before the time of the meeting of the electors, Greeley died. The sixty-six electors who presumably otherwise would have voted for him cast their votes for a number of other individuals, except three in Georgia who voted for Greeley anyway. The Congress accepted the votes cast for the others, but would not record the three Georgia votes for Greeley on the ground that they were not cast for a person!

Years later, in 1912, although involving the vote for vice-president, the votes of eight electors which ordinarily would have been cast for Republican candidate James Sherman were cast for Nicholas Murray Butler. Sherman had died before the electoral college met. Presumably these electors did so with the precedent of the Greeley vote in Georgia.

40

These defections made no difference in the outcome, but if the division of the total national
electoral vote had been extremely narrow different
results might have been obtained.

The 1968 election gives some support for retention
of the person of elector. Prior to election day there
were indications that neither Nixon nor Humphrey would
receive a majority of the electoral vote, since it was
assumed that Wallace would gain the vote of a number
of Southern states, which he did. Without a majority
vote in the electoral college the decision would
automatically be shifted to the House of Representatives. This prospect was viewed by some as a possible
chamber of horrors with estimates of bargaining evils
among House members and the candidates involved.

George Wallace, the possible election "spoiler",
took a different view and is quoted as having said that
he believed the decision would be made in the electoral
college notwithstanding the prospect that neither Nixon
nor Humphrey appeared to have a majority--before the
actual electoral college vote. This was his explanation given prior to election day.[2]

Question. If none of the three candidates
get a majority, is the election going to be
decided in the Electoral College or in the House
of Representatives?

Wallace. I think it would be settled in the
Electoral College.

Question. Two of the candidates get together
or their electors get together and determine who
is to be President?

Wallace. That is right.

Apparently Wallace believed that agreements
favorable to some of his views could be realized in
that way than if attempted in the House. If so, the
terms of any agreements would be among the three candidates or two of them and the needed number of electors.
Who other "actors" might have been may remain a
mystery.

Not only was the prospect of selection of a president by the House unacceptable to defector Dr. Bailey
and to Wallace, other electors had considered having
the decision made without resort to the House if a

majority vote in the electoral college was not realized by the apparent election day decision. In his "Presidential Lottery" James Michener, an elector on the Democratic slate in Pennsylvania, wrote that he and others, at least in that state, would have cast their votes for the plurality national popular vote winner if there was no presumed majority in the electoral college vote. Michener made it clear that the object was to prevent bargaining of any kind either in or out of the electoral college thereby including the House.

The question can be raised, in view of the above, whether there is some positive value in retaining the person of elector. The Michener or even the Bailey position suggests an added contingency method, but had that occurred in 1968 it might not have had an automatic acceptance in the Congress.

Obviously, had the 1968 election resulted in no winner and the automatic plan had been in effect the decision would have had to go the House. It is at best speculative to have predicted what the House decision would have been. It might have been to support the national popular vote plurality winner even without the fearsome bargaining.

In its most simple form, the automatic plan does not disturb the House contingency feature. If the person of the elector was eliminated there would need to be some contingency plan. Assuming the prospective evils of election in the House, a shift to the automatic plan could also include some other arrangement. Possibilities include (retaining the House as the forum since it would provide a "fresh" expression of the voters but modify it to authorize one vote for each House member rather than a state by state vote.) This proposal does not eliminate the prospects of bargaining, to be sure, but it would presumably end the possibility of a tie vote--although it would not guarantee it--and it would end the disparity of having each state's delegation producing one vote each and the resulting disparity mentioned earlier.

This contingency arrangement would not be wholly acceptable to those adhering to a federal design for electing the president since the states, as states, would not be fully recognized. Another alternative to the present one would be to have the decision made by a joint session of the Congress with each Representative and Senator having one vote.

Other alternatives are to provide that the winner be the popular vote plurality victor (if no popular vote majority for any candidate) or to have a popular runoff election between the two top popular vote recipients or even the two with the highest electoral vote.

Some objections to any contingency plan involving selection by either or both houses of the Congress is that its use infringes on the doctrine of the separation of powers and would make the president so selected too dependent on the legislative branch or some of its membership. A continuing objection for a decision in the House is that even with each member having one vote it would still violate the principle of equal population ratios not only because of the more favorable vote weight for small states but for most elections numerous House members would not represent equal population ratios since they are derived from the decennial census and therefore out of date. Any plan which also includes an equal vote in a joint session is considered by some to be faulty since it would reflect the "constant two" electoral advantage for many states. Egalitarians also observe that up to two-thirds of the Senate membership would be holdovers and not reflect any fresh mandate from the voters.

Opponents of the electoral college system do not find much consolation in the automatic plan. As the 1977 Senate Committee on the Judiciary Report put it, "The elector is to the body politic what the appendix is to the human body. As Henry Cabot Lodge said, 'While it does no good and ordinarily causes no trouble, it continually exposes the body to the danger of political peritonitus! We can avoid this potentially dangerous disease by eliminating the elector. But that is not a cure-all for what ails our present electoral machinery'".[3]

The Proportional Plan.

This plan would continue the present allocation of electoral votes. But all electoral votes would be assigned on an at-large basis and without the person of the elector. Each candidate for president would receive a percentage of the electoral vote based on his proportion of the total popular vote cast in each state.

This method was proposed in the Congress more than a century ago. In its original form each state's vote would be rounded off to whole numbers, but since that time, partly because of close elections, proportional plans would require the division be done by decimals to the nearest one-thousandths of an electoral vote.

Recent proposals under the plan would make the plurality winner the president, if there was no majority decision, providing the plurality reached at least 40% of the electoral vote nationwide. If not, the election would be made under a contingency plan by members of the House and Senate, meeting jointly, with each member having one vote. A majority of those present and voting would be required.

Under the proportional plan the electors would not be retained. Thus, (the faithless elector would no longer be a factor.) Furthermore, (all electoral votes allocated to a state would be divided according to the total popular votes cast and the division would thereby closely reflect the proportion of popular votes cast for each candidate in each state.) One version of the plan would allocate all of the votes based on the constant-two to the nationwide plurality winner of the total national popular vote, providing there was no clear majority winner of that vote. Translated into whole numbers this would affect 102 votes, two of which are the ones allocated to the District of Columbia.

(This plan would encourage two-party competition if none existed and would also very likely encourage third or splinter parties to field candidates.) Since the unit rule would end for votes based on House membership and for all unless the alternate plan was used for the votes based on the Senate. States previously considered "safe" for a political party much of the time would be diminished or even ended. A Republican candidate, for example, would reasonably expect some percentage of the electoral vote in the District! Supporters of this plan believe that voter turnout would increase since the electoral vote allocation would be in proportion to the votes for each candidate. Although methods for handling challenges, based on real or alleged fraud or counting errors, may require a complete state-by-state overhaul, proponents state that the impact of fraud would be minimal since small margins would be affected and not large blocs of votes which electoral college critics say can prevail widely at present.

A major criticism of the electoral college system

is that it provides a built-in advantage to large organized majorities and to states with large metropolitan areas wherein bloc voting may often occur. Advocates of the proportional plan insist that this would be reduced substantially or even eliminated to the point of little advantage to such blocs. That is not to state that bloc voting would end, but rather that any relative advantage under the unit rule would be curtailed.

In a sense, (the proportional plan can be considered as a compromise between the present electoral college system and direct national popular election.) The relative voting strength for the candidates would more nearly reflect the final tabulations, albeit in a decimal system. It should more nearly reflect also the total national candidate vote results even including the two-at-large votes however allocated.

This plan is corrective in some respects but does not preclude the election of a candidate who did not receive a majority or plurality of the total national popular vote. (Critics of the plan express concern also that it would have serious adverse effects on the two-party system since it would encourage third party) splinter, or "spoiler" party activity and would more likely mean frequent use of the contingency plan. The experience in the 1968 and 1980 elections would suggest that the time may have passed anyway when the two major parties can prevent third parties from making inroads of consequence in election contests.

Democratic purists quickly point out that the plan continues the hated votes based on the "constant two" of the Senate and thereby thwarts the national will. Although the design of the plan is not rooted in the total national popular vote, critics indicate that it would be completely intolerable for a winner not to have at least a plurality of the total national popular vote.

If the proportional plan required a minimum electoral vote, perhaps as much as 40 percent, and the highest vote did not reach that level, then some contingency arrangement would become operative. One has been suggested above. Another is to continue the present House plan, but that might be of doubtful acceptance since it is based on conditions of state by state equality. Another is to use a runoff between the two top candidates.

There are opposing views whether the proportional plan would be more easily understood by the voter than the present electoral college system. The present use of whole numbers is a marked contrast to a decimal system. Critics abound who insist that the plan falls short of meeting a very basic requirement, that of voter and vote equality.

In their analysis of the proportional plan, Wallace S. Sayre and Judith H. Parris emphasize the plan's political implications and that it would severely check the existing power of major metropolitan areas. They express concern that "the internal solidarity" of some states would make them greater political prizes. They further believe that the metropolitan areas of the most populous states would lose the potential power they might have or already have under the general ticket system and as a result "all other areas would stand to gain." Major beneficiaries would be small town, rural, and suburban areas, especially those with significant one-party strength.[4]

It should not necessarily be concluded from a reading of that appraisal that the authors oppose the consequences, but rather suggest that a decline of the political power of these metropolitan centers would have major political policy implications. They believe that the proportional plan would also assist more conservative elements of the population. If the general-ticket or unit rule were ended they indicate that the voters in those states which have been more solidly Republican would cause conservative elements within that party to be more powerful than in the past. They suggest further that the Republican party would be more likely to nominate a candidate less "attuned to minority group concerns, and possibly less internationalist than most of the candidates have been in the past."

Would the use of the proportional plan mean that the Democratic party would continue to have large city domination and retain so-called Democratic states, too? If so, it would cause the party's presidential candidate to be liberal on such matters as welfare, oriented toward policy concerns of many urban based groups and to use the phrase from Sayre and Parris, to be "at least cautiously internationalist as well." One problem for the Democrats would be to make stronger appeals to some of the smaller, less populus states which might be more politically homogenous. Appeals to the voters in them would need to be somewhat different,

46

however, than to voters in the large urban areas as these analysts view the matter.

In his testimony before the Senate Subcommittee on Constitutional Amendments in 1969 Professor Malcolm Jewell of the University of Kentucky made this observation:

> The reason why the proportional and district plans are both doomed to defeat needs to be stressed. Both plans would clearly transfer political power away from major groups of voters in the nation, while giving a clear advantage enjoyed by large states in the present bloc-voting system and give the small states (and those with low turnout) an advantage under the electoral college formula for apportioning votes. Consequently the large states will vigorously oppose both the proportional and district plans.[5]

Ziedenstein observes that under these two plans a state would be able to cast its full electoral vote regardless of the size of the popular vote, presumably meaning that in those states with a low voter turnout there would be a comparative distortion with states having a high turnout. This argument, in turn, is used to support the direct national popular vote plan.

The proportional plan undoubtedly would subject the two major parties to challenges by splinter groups with a chance of any reasonable showing. As indicated above they would receive some fraction of the electoral vote regardless of the popular vote received. At present many party dissidents remain nominally in a major party simply because they have no place to go.

The Federal Plan.

This plan was recommended to the Senate Judiciary Committee in 1970 by Senator Thomas F. Eagleton, Democrat of Missouri, and Senator Robert Dole, Republican of Kansas. It seems to have been born of response to criticisms of the direct national popular vote plan then under active consideration by that Committee.

The federal plan would provide for the election of a plurality winner if there was no majority in a national popular vote, providing the candidate won in more than half of the states or had a plurality in states with over half the voters, or if the candidate won a majority of the electoral votes based on the general ticket unit rule.) If there still was no winner, then any electoral votes won by minor party candidates would be shifted and allocated to the two top contenders in proportion to their vote in each state thereby making one of the two major-party candidates the winner.

This plan, obviously somewhat complex, (seems to be aimed at the influence third or minor parties might have and the scheme to shift their votes would prevent one of their candidates from having enough strength to win the election.)

The Senators apparently believed that the plan would not require a contingency feature such as action by the House or a joint session or for a national popular vote runoff. The reallocation of votes would not make that necessary.

The federal plan has found few supporters. It does combine some features of other plans, including some from the present supporters of the electoral college system, but it would likely be strongly opposed by most egalitarians.

(The Tydings-Griffin Plan)

This plan also stems from consideration of the direct national popular vote proposal. It was offered by Senator Joseph D. Tydings, Democrat of Maryland, and Senator Robert P. Griffin, Republican of Michigan. Essentially, (it provides that if no candidate received at least a 40 percent plurality of the total national popular vote, then a majority of electoral votes, allocated on the present formula, would determine the election.) But if the use of the electoral vote did not produce a winner, then a contingency would be used in the form of a joint session of the Congress with each member having one vote. The intent is that if the contingency feature was used the vote would have to be a majority to have a winner. The 40 percent popular vote feature suggests that another alternative would be a national runoff between the two contenders.

As with the federal plan, the Tydings-Griffin plan has attracted few supporters. This brief mention of it here is to reflect the concerns of some members of the Congress over the possible destruction of the electoral college system but also to offer some changes in it without catipulting it into oblivion.

The Spong Proposal.

Another hybrid proposal was presented by Senator William B. Spong, Jr., Democrat of Virginia. Its design provides that to win a candidate would need to receive an electoral majority as at present, but also would have to attain at least a plurality of the total national popular vote. If both of these conditions were not met, then the selection would be made by a joint session of the Congress as provided in some other contingency proposals. There seems to have been little interest in this proposal.

In either of the above plans, the Tydings-Griffin and Spong, the contingency feature for a decision by the Congress could mean a president would be selected who was not the candidate who received the most popular votes or the most votes in the electoral college. Of course, the candidate having a national plurality might not win under the electoral college system.

These latter plans do not indicate any need for the person of elector. As presented neither included a plan for a runoff contingency. The runoff in a second national contest is intended to strike at the use of the Congress in any fashion.

The Bonus Plan.

This plan is the newest entry. Called by some an ingenious one, it introduces a new element in the presidential selection process. It appears to rest on a desire to retain the essentials of the present allocation of electoral college votes, state by state, but adds on another 102 votes. That number, obviously is arrived at from the total of the votes based on Senate membership plus the two for the District.

These 102 added votes would be cast automatically for the candidate having the highest total national popular vote. The person of elector would be eliminated thus assuming some features of the automatic plan.

The plan provides for a contingency in the event no candidate received a majority of the 640 electoral votes. This addition of the 102 votes recognizes the prospect of one or more third parties whose candidates would receive some electoral votes and enough to prevent a majority as is possible at present. The

49

contingency is for a runoff nationally between the two candidates receiving the most popular votes similar to other runoff proposals. Supporters of this plan would also include features to speed the counting of the vote to avoid the prospect of not reaching a decision on time if the contingency was necessary.

Advocates of this plan claim that it provides for the essentials of the direct vote plan and does it in an acceptable way. Critics quickly observe that it is a "gimmick" with direct vote underpinnings. Another analysis states that since "it is virtually impossible to contemplate the bonus plan selecting a minority President, one is hard-pressed to figure out why one needs the system at all."[6]

The District Plan.

The district plan does not disturb the method of allocating electoral votes to the states. Depending upon the version of the plan, it could or could not retain the person of elector. Also depending on the version, the contingency plan would provide for any of those already associated with other plans. Earlier versions have included retention of the present House feature or to substitute the idea of a joint session. The runoff feature could be an alternative, including the 40 percent popular vote plurality requirement.

The most distinctive feature of the plan is the allocation of one electoral vote to each electoral district in each state. It is generally assumed that these districts would be the same as the seats for the House. They could be different. The two votes based on Senate membership would be general ticket or at-large votes. The vote in each district would go to the plurality winner if there was no majority and the candidate receiving the highest vote on a state-wide basis would receive the two at-large votes. (This is the arrangement presently in Maine, and an analysis of the Maine plan follows this general presentation of the district plan).

Some versions of the district plan are designed to restrict the possibility of political gerrymandering of electoral districts by the state legislatures. Unquestionably the prospect of gerrymandering looms high among critics of the plan. To prevent such possibilities, some have urged that strict standards be imposed for the setting of boundaries including placing the responsibility in some public commission

50

independent of the legislature. The concerns are at least threefold--disparities in population, dilution of minority strengths, and political partisanship. Where prevailing, any one of these issues could form the basis of lengthy litigation. These prospects exist at present for House districts and have been the subject of judicial contests as well in the state legislatures.

The district plan is one of the oldest of the proposals advanced for changing the method of electing the president. It seems to be the plan favored by James Madison. According to his correspondence, he asserted that it was the intention "of those who framed and ratified the Constitution that the electors would be chosen within their respective districts, rather than in statewide elections."

The district plan was used in several states in the early years. By 1836 only South Carolina retained it and abandoned it in favor of the general-ticket system in 1860. The abandonments were based primarily on the belief that the mixed pattern between the district method and the unit rule diluted party strength in the states having the district plan. Political leaders believed the statewide single slate was the most advantageous.

Several times during the first half of the 19th century the plan was presented to the Congress as a proposed Constitutional amendment. It was approved several times in the Senate and barely failed of the required vote in the House during the same period.

Subsequently the plan had little national or congressional attention until after World War II. Since that time it has had varying amounts of support and was advanced on occasion as the best alternative to other plans and especially to the national popular vote proposal. More recently, however, it has lost much of its congressional support and was given little attention during the 1979 Senate hearings.

The plan is easily understood since the electoral votes continue to be assigned to each state as at present and add the ingredient of one vote for each local (district) area.

Proponents of the district plan emphasize that one of the major defects of the present electoral college system is that an advantage is given to larger, often

to states with narrow political divisions, and this is
grossly unfair. The adoption of the district arrangement would greatly diminish that claimed advantage.
Supporters also state that in those states having
a history of generally favoring the candidate of a
particular political party would find that under the
plan two-party competition would increase and encourage much higher voter participation. Critics respond
saying that the district plan would encourage third
or splinter and "spoiler" party candidates, making it
difficult to have the vote reflect the popular will.
The plurality candidate might actually have a very low
proportion of the total popular vote in a given district. Proponents discount this as highly unlikely
since minor party candidates would have to demonstrate
substantial strength to win enough votes to be a
threat to either of the two major party-candidates.

One concern about all proposed alternatives to
changing the method of electing the president which is
frequently voiced by defenders of the present system
is the prospect of any change would include or at
least encourage the total nationalization of the
nominating and election process. State laws would be
supplanted through congressional pre-emption of election administration. Supporters of the district plan
do not appear to envision that prospect.

An analysis of any proposal must include reference
to election challenges especially when due to fraud or
claims of fraud. Challenges to the election outcome
are not unusual in the United States whether for
electoral votes or for an office in the lowest governmental hierarchy. Supporters of the district plan
believe that with more localized controls inherent in
the plan the chances of fraud would not be great and
if there was it would not affect the final outcome,
whereas under the present general-ticket system the
possibilities could be much greater. Of greater concern may be the highly diverse methods among the
states for handling disputes, and in a close election,
such as in 1960, a final decision might be delayed for
many months.

As with the proportional plan, the district plan
is challenged for its possible impact on the political
strategy in presidential nominations and campaigns.
A state which presently is likely to deliver its
electoral vote to a particular candidate would have,
or might have, that vote divided. In his appraisal,
Sindler suggests that under the plan districts which

were highly competitive, for example, would receive "disproportionate attention but their interests and policy concerns could differ markedly from those of pivotal states as generally prevails presently." He also states that the willingness of some proponents of the plan to accept a compromise by including the 40% popular vote rule is an indication, perhaps an admission that the plan "would mean a greater potential for third parties" than under the present electoral college system.[7]

There is diverse opinion whether the district plan would adversely affect the doctrine of the separation of powers and thereby place too much dependency of presidential candidates on successes in House districts, assuming the electoral districts coincided with them. Some candidates for the House have not always given open support to the presidential candidate of their party and on occasion a presidential candidate has, in effect, been virtually invited to stay away. Sindler raises the question, however, whether in the long-run House candidacies might become adjuncts of the presidential contest each four years.

One of the most detailed considerations of the district plan in concept is by Sayre and Parris.[8] Their first concern is that the district plan would significantly alter the constituency base of the president because of the change in the selection of electors and the final allocation of votes. To them there would be an end to the preferred position of the more populous states. The smaller states and regions outside metropolitan areas would assume much of that advantage. They assert that "presidential politics would be localized," since only two of a state's electoral votes would be determined on a statewide basis, except, of course, in those states having but one House seat. In arithmetic total there are 108 such votes. Conversely, 80 percent of the electoral vote would be determined by the vote in the localized districts.

Assuming the relative correctness of the Sayre and Parris position, the district plan advances the idea of equality within the states and reduces the political advantage the general-ticket or unit rule may give to the more populous states. The question remains, however, whether there should be greater concern over any shift of political power for the presidency from those states since it can be argued that in so doing the more "liberal" elements in them would suffer

53

a decline. Those supporting that view indicate that the district system would end the "strategic importance" of major suburban areas which also have a present considerable advantage. Not all suburban areas would be similarly affected, however. Those whose "interests allied them more often with core-city areas would tend to lose; suburbs in less populous states and those allied more frequently with small towns and rural areas would similarly gain."[9]

Would these changes, if they came about, alter the policy orientation of a presidential incumbent? Questions are raised also about a possible decline in the influence of some ethnic groups--as were raised about the proportional plan--on the nation's foreign policy. Would the trend result generally in a president being less hawkish and more restrained and one tending toward isolation?

Sayre and Parris point out that the district plan would "tend to make the major parties less heterogeneous."[10] Would it increase party competition? Advocates say, yes. But would the races in the electoral districts be more or less evenly divided than at present? Many House districts are not really competitive at present. Would the district system alter that and correspondingly alter the presidential elector vote? Could political gerrymandering be successfully insulated against? These writers believe the district plan would give an overall assist in strengthening the Republican party. They also emphasize that since every voter would be able to cast three votes for electors, voting habits would not be altered significantly and the relative voting power of each voter would be more nearly equalized than at present. Advocates of the plan believe this would occur, but this is not easily proven.

One of the criticisms leveled at the general-ticket arrangement is that all votes in a given state are given to the majority or plurality winner, statewide. Under the district system, obviously, some of the same conditions would prevail except that the focal point for the prospective winner would be on each district and not just the statewide votes which would be reduced to two, save in the small states. This historical argument over the "taking away" of votes for the loser and giving them to the winner would be of no more significance than at present since there is but one winner. In contrast to the proportional plan there is no splitting of a vote.

54

The post-election exercise to re-shape the election outcome would not end under the district plan. Raw election data can show, for example, that the presidential winner now might have been a runner-up if the national popular vote is used to show it. But these arithmetic exercises seem to assume that under the district plan all other things would have been equal. This assumption is questionable for they would not have been equal. Thus, the shifting of results from the one to the other can be only illustrative.

The general-ticket system is further criticized since in its use there can be a delay in determining the winner in a close election. Undoubtedly under the district plan a similar circumstance could arise. But then the decision does not have to be determined on election night.

Opponents of the district plan predict a changing of the "shape of the presidency" in its use, since, they insist, the president would be selected under a contingency plan more often than infrequently. This is in the belief that a shift to more localized voting would mean much closer elections than in past close ones. And if an election becomes "too close to call" before or even after the election, and the decision was made in the House or both houses, the candidates for the presidency would be unlikely to present very divergent views, especially for the two major-party candidates. Would this result from forcing the candidates to place greater emphasis on local issues to gain district support? Would state legislatures face even greater conflicts in the decennial re-drawing of districts?

Sayre and Parris conclude their analysis of the district plan with this observation. "The district plan must be considered to be more than a remedy for the supposed defects of the electoral college system. It is really a protest against the sort of presidency that has developed during the twentieth century."[11] That would seem to be an overly broad conclusion.

The analysis of the district plan by Longley and Braun produces few features about the impact from its use beyond those already presented. They address the prospect of fraud, however, which they believe could be magnified "in swing or marginal districts where shifts of relatively small numbers of votes could determine entire blocs of electoral votes." They also express concern about the disparity in the

allocation of votes which might result from out-of-date
census data. That there could be some changes in
population which need to be corrected more frequently
is not disputed, but this argument is used primarily
to advance the national popular vote plan. These
writers also observe that the district plan would
continue the defect of a possible winner of the presidency who did not also have the plurality of the total
nationwide popular vote. Advocates of the district
plan do not dispute that prospect.[12]

Zeidenstein virtually dismisses the district plan
as having little worth in an exceedingly brief commentary.[13]

The district plan is presently functioning, as
already indicated, though only in the state of Maine.
It was first in place for the 1972 presidential election. The development of the Maine plan and its
operation should serve to demonstrate its possible
application in other states.

The Maine district arrangement began on January 8,
1969 when State Representative S. Glenn Starbird, Jr.,
of Kingman Township, Penobscot County, Maine, introduced H. P. 74. Originally styled as "An Act Dividing
the State of Maine into Presidential Election
Districts," the legislation later to become control-
ling and beginning with the 1972 election, made Maine
the first state in this century to change from the
blanket ticket or winner-take-all plan for selecting
presidential electors.

The original proposal by Representative Starbird
would have divided the state into four districts.
Maine has two House districts. In committee, however,
the proposal was modified to conform to the arrangement which has been known traditionally as the "District
Plan", one which provides for at-large and district
electors. The Legislative Committee on State
Government redrafted the measure and reported it to
the full chamber, without dissent, on February 20,
1969. It was entitled "An Act Relating to Presidential
Electors at Large and From Districts."

The text of the measure is as follows:

Section 1181-A. There shall be chosen a Presidential Elector from each congressional district
and 2 at large.
Section 1-A. The Presidential Electors at large

shall cast their ballots for President and Vice-President of the political party which received the largest number of votes in the State. The Electors of each congressional district shall cast their ballots for President and Vice-President of the political party which received the largest number of votes in each congressional district.

Favorable action, without dissent, took place in the House of Representatives on March 6, 1969, and after similar action in the Senate, it was signed by the President of the Senate on March 19, 1969, and sent to the Governor.

Of special interest is the apparent ease with which the measure made its way through the Maine legislature. There was no organized opposition or effort to promote its passage. Representative Starbird argued that the direct popular election of the President, then under active consideration by the Congress, should be avoided. He considered national popular election to be destructive of the American federal system, and argued that its adoption would seriously and adversely affect the role of political parties in the states and highly detrimental to the Constitutional arrangement which he believed provides for a "federal" president. He maintained that the District plan was designed to correct some defects in the prevailing electoral college general ticket system, and indeed, that the District plan was what the framers of the Constitution had intended.

During the legislative journey toward passage, Mr. Starbird was asked by some individuals, both in and out of the legislature, to withdraw his proposal. This opposition apparently was based on concern that any Maine favorite son seeking the presidential nomination should not have to face the prospect of having one possible electoral vote cast against him if he was nominated by his party in a national convention. But the opposition was too little and too late. The measure previously had received the open endorsement of the legislative leadership in both houses of the Maine legislature and remained firm.

Governor Kenneth M. Curtis, a Democrat, did not sign the measure and it became law without his approval. It was reported at the time that the Governor had indicated he would examine the proposal and before taking any action he would advise, informally, his proposed action. Reports also circulated that the Governor was strongly urged by some fellow Democrats to veto the measure, but he had earlier informally assured the legislative leadership that he would not exercise the veto and he honored that commitment.

The legislative record included the following commentary about the District plan when it was before the Senate on March 11, 1969. Senator Bennett D. Katz, Republican, of Kennebec County, said:[14]

> Mr. President, I would like to call the Senate's attention to this bill. Earlier in this session the Senate passed to be engrossed a measure which I sponsored which would seek to bind the presidential electors to vote for the candidate of their own party. This bill does something that I think no other state in the country has done yet, and I think it is a very, very good piece of legislation. Actually it is our first attempt to go in the direction of popular election of the president of the United States.
>
> While Congress is groping with the problem of how to do it on a national basis, you will notice that this bill actually makes it possible for one candidate of the other party to get one electoral vote. From the Republican point of view, this means that in a Democratic sweep we can still salvage one of the electoral votes, and the opposite is also true. I note this came out of committee unanimously Ought to Pass, so probably it is a good thing for both parties.

One of the early arguments in favor of the blanket rule was that while it consolidates the electoral vote, the district plan disperses the vote. This is true, of course, but as Senator Katz observed, the district plan formally recognizes voter decisions for a portion of the electoral vote if enough voters in a state so decide. The blanket ticket does not. In 1976, for example, with a shift of only a few hundred votes in the Second district, Carter would have been allocated one of the state's electoral votes. But as with most attempts to re-create an election after the event, that surmise is but an indication that the district plan recognizes a strong minority of voters who can become a majority.

A long-standing argument against the district plan is that it weakens the two-party system. In the 1972 election in Maine, there were no minor parties on the presidential ballot and Nixon carried the two Districts--and therefore the state--by overwhelming majorities.[15] In the 1976 election the situation was different. There were four presidential candidates on the ballot: Ford, Carter, McCarthy, and Bubar. (Benjamin C. Bubar was the national candidate for the Prohibition Party, and also a Maine resident). Ford carried the First district by 3,421 votes but McCarthy (Eugene J. McCarthy, formerly Democratic Senator from Wisconsin) tallied 6,025 and Bubar 1,281. In the Second district, Ford carried the District by a margin of only 620 votes. McCarthy was supported by 4,849 voters and Bubar by 2,214. An argument could be made that without McCarthy being on the ballot in the First district, Carter would have received enough of McCarthy's votes to have carried it and if neither McCarthy or Bubar had been on the ballot, Carter would have carried the Second district also and therefore the state to receive its four electoral votes.

Did the district plan foster and nourish this minority party activity? The view that it did falls far short of evidence needed to support that claim. McCarthy was a spoiler in similar circumstances in several other states in 1976 and especially in Oregon, Oklahoma, and Iowa, where Ford won the electoral vote by small margins over Carter. McCarthy's place on the Maine ballot was not an isolated situation.

A related claim against the district plan is that it encourages a presidential campaign which over-emphasizes local issues and tends to highlight them over broader regional and national matters. There is little evidence in 1972, 1976 or in 1980 that local matters received more than scant attention in either Maine district by the candidates or their supporters. For example, Carter was in Maine only once in the fall of 1976 and appeared in Portland before a samll audience. Mondale appeared in Lewiston (Second district) and Dole came once to Portland (First district) and Bangor (Second district). Maine political observers do not believe that local issues mattered at all in the campaigning or the voting. There was some effort by state groups supporting major party candidates, but their activity appears to have been mainly to "get out the vote" rather than about any Ford or Carter positions on local matters.

In the 1980 election there were six candidates on the ballot. In addition to Carter and Republican

Ronald Reagan, candidates included Ed Clark, Libertarian Party, John Anderson, Independent Party, Gus Hall, Communist Party, and Barry Commoner, Citizens Party.

In the First district, Reagan received 126,274 votes, Carter 117,613, and Anderson 30,889. The other candidates received 5,694 votes. If pre-election assumptions were generally correct, and Anderson had not been on the ballot, and if his supporters were mostly otherwise inclined toward Carter, Carter would have carried that district.

In the Second district, Reagan received 112,248 votes, Carter 103,361, and Anderson 22,438. Again, if most of the Anderson votes otherwise had gone to Carter, absent Anderson on the ballot, Carter would have carried that district also, and thereby received all four of the state's electoral votes. The records for the 1980 and the 1976 elections are similar in this respect. Anderson received enough votes in several states to suggest that had he not been on the ballot Carter would have carried them. These included Arkansas, Delaware, Massachusetts, Michigan, New York, Tennessee, Vermont, and Wisconsin. However, even if all of these states had shifted to Carter, Reagan still would have won the election.

It is alleged that the district plan has an inherent weakness since the districts would be drawn by the state legislature and therefore automatically subject to political gerrymandering. In Maine, the U. S. House districts are also the presidential electoral districts. But that arrangement was by the overwhelming choice of the legislature. As a result of the 1960 census of population Maine lost one of its (then) three House seats. In redistricting the state into two districts, the Republican controlled legislature placed the predominately Democratic Androscoggin County in the Second district in the hope that this action would give the Republican party an advantage in the new First district. In subsequent elections, however, the results have not supported any particular advantage to Republican candidates.

Alghough comparable data are not readily available for all of the states, Maine's political party memberships or "party enrollments" are somewhat distinctive due to the large number of independent voters. Data for party affiliation in 1972, for example, shows eligible Republican voters over Democrats and the 1976 data indicate an advantage for Republicans in the

First district and for the Democrats in the Second.
These data do not include independents or those who
did not at the time register their political preference.
For the 1976 presidential election the independents
accounted for nearly thirty percent of the total vote
in the First district and more than twenty-five percent
in the Second. Enrollments with the Democratic party
and the Republican party were nearly equal in the
state as a whole.

For the 1980 election, the Democrats enrolled
voters with a slightly greater number than Republicans
in the First district, but a strong numerical advantage
over Republicans in the Second. In 1980, independents
accounted for nearly 300,000 of the 760,000 voters and
those registered to vote. The total vote for all
presidential electors for all candidates was about 69
percent of the total.

Thus, whether possible gerrymandering accomplished
its original purpose or not, it is clouded by the large
number of independents. In 1976 the popular vote for
Ford in the First district was 127,019 to 123,598 for
Carter. In the Second district the results were
109,301 for Ford and 108,681 for Carter. It is apparent
that party workers in both of the major parties had not
only to try to hold their enrolled voters, but also to
seek vigorously the support of many independents.

Similar results are reflected in the 1980 election.
The Republican House candidate for the First district
won by 188,667 to 86,819 for the Democrat. In the
Second district the Republican House candidate won by
even greater support, 186,406 to 51,026.

An assumption about the district plan has been
that its use would weaken the Presidency by making it
more dependent on the Congress since the districts
for the electoral vote would likely be the same as for
House districts, as they are in Maine. But in 1976,
for example, the results in the two House districts do
not appear to support this contention. In the First
district the Republican candidate won by 145,523 to
108,105 for his Democratic opponent. The Second
district was also won by a Republican with 169,292 to
43,150. It should be noted that Second district Republican Representative William S. Cohen actively
campaigned for Ford, but as shown above Ford's margin
was only a few hundred votes over Carter. Had Cohen
not made a special effort for Ford, Carter might have
carried the Second district.

(Another claimed disadvantage of the district plan is that the winner of the popular vote could lose the presidency in the electoral college.) Of course this could happen as it could under the blanket ticket system.

Another criticism of the district plan is that it would favor Republicans over Democrats. The Maine experience in the last three presidential elections do not support the argument. With voter enrollments about evenly divided between Republicans and Democrats in 1976 and with the Democrats having an advantage in 1980 by more than 10 percent, there is strong two-party activity in the state. The closeness of the results in the presidential elections is evidence. Interestingly, the governor of Maine elected in 1976 was an Independent.

(Another argument against the district plan is that it isolates minorities and disperses their strength and possible voter advantage.) The elections under the district plan in Maine do not support that claim.

Observers close to the recent presidential elections in Maine believe that the overwhelming majority of Maine voters gave almost no attention to the existence of the district plan. It was of some interest by party workers for Carter in the 1976 election since some of them (and some elsewhere) believed the election would be so close that a single electoral vote might determine the outcome and Maine was the only place where one vote could be isolated.

Supporters of the direct vote plan amay not agree with Maine State Senator Katz that the district plan is a step in that direction, but those who find the popular election plan the most acceptable, indeed the only alternative to the electoral college as it prevails now, save in Maine, should examine more fully the Maine experience with the district plan before endowing the nation with a far more drastic change in the method of electing the president of the United States.

Attention is concentrated on the direct vote plan in the following chapter.

Presidential Elections of 1960 and 1968
Comparative Results under Present and Proposed Systems

1960

Candidate	Total popular vote	Electoral College	Proportional	District
Nixon	34,108,546	219	263.632	278
Kennedy	34,221,349	303	262.671	245
Unpledged	609,870	15	8.627	14

1968

Nixon	31,770,237	301	231.534	289
Humphrey	31,270,533	191	225.362	192
Wallace	9,897,146	46	79.455	57
Others	239,910		1.605	

With a minimum of 270 electoral votes needed, the 1960 election would have been decided by the House of Representatives under the proportional plan if the plan stipulated that a majority of "whole" numbers was needed. Nixon had a plurality but not a majority of the entire electoral college. Under the district plan Nixon would have been the winner notwithstanding the lower total national popular vote. Similar conclusions can be drawn about the proportional and district plans for the 1968 election

FOOTNOT

63

1. U.S. Congress, Senate, Judiciary Committee, Sub-committee on Constitutional Amendments, Hearings on Electing the President, 91st Cong., 1st sess., January 23 and 24, March 10, 11, 12, 13, 20, and 21, April 30, May 1 and 2, 1969, pp. 36-41.

2. U. S. News and World Report, September 30, 1968, p. 34

3. U. S. Congress, Senate, Judiciary Committee, Report on Direct Popular Election of the President and Vice President of the United States, 95th Cong., 1st sess., Report 95-609, December 6, 1977, p. 8.

4. Op. cit., Ch. VII.

5. 1969 Senate Hearings, p. 477.

6. Arrington, Theodore S., and Saul Brenner, "The Advantages of a Plurality Election of the President," Presidential Studies Quarterly, v. X, no. 3, Summer 1980, p. 486.

7. Op. cit., p. 58.

8. Op. cit., p. 104.

9. Ibid., p. 107.

10. Ibid., p. 108.

11. Ibid., p. 117.

12. Op. cit., p. 63.

13. Op. cit., p. 17.

14. Maine Legislative Record, Senate, March 11, 1969, p. 538.

15. Election data obtained courtesy the Office of the Secretary of State for Maine.

Advocates of the direct national popular vote plan believed that notwithstanding defeat through inaction in the Senate in 1969 after overwhelming approval by the House that year, the plan would be approved by both houses of the Congress and ratified by the required majority of the state legislatures during the 1970s. That optimism was not realized, of course, when the plan was defeated in the Senate on July 10, 1979.

Although ultimate success in the not too distant future seems to be the goal of its supporters, the timetable for achieving that hope is uncertain. Equally uncertain is whether the Senate defeat will be considered not more than a skirmish and an element only of delay or whether the defeat will prompt some reorientation of the extreme change the direct vote plan would make in the election of the president. Supporters of the plan were encouraged that it would receive congressional support as alternatives to it gradually lost support. Indeed, the debates and hearings increasingly focused almost wholly on the issue whether the direct vote plan should be adopted or whether the present electoral college system should continue. Other plans were, in effect, virtually blacked out. Whether there will be a resurgence of support for one of them or some new combination remains to be seen. Certainly if there is another close election in the electoral college or one which requires the use of the House contingency plan it is likely there will be a clamor to change the system. The success of the electoral college in 1980 may also serve to dampen early efforts for change. Furthermore, the most ardent and continuing champion of the direct vote plan in the Senate during the 1970s was Senator Birch Bayh, Democrat of Indiana, and he was defeated in his bid for re-election in 1980.

Zeidenstein put the matter of an early effort to pursue the direct vote plan in this way: ". . . on the day the Electoral College goes awry--when it 'elects' as President the candidate who polled second place in popular votes, or when a regional party prevents any candidate from winning a majority of electoral votes and the election is decided either by bargaining for minor party electors or in the House of Representatives, with each delegation casting one vote--on that day public opinion will <u>demand</u> passage of

65

a direct election amendment."[1]

It may be observed that if those conditions arose the bargaining for electoral votes need not be restricted to minor party candidates, or their electors.

The "direct vote plan" is a shortened and somewhat misleading label for it. To use either the term "direct election" or "direct vote" only is to ignore or possibly submerge the nature of the plan in one vital respect: it is a national vote plan and removes all vestiges of the federal design, save perhaps the possibility that the states would continue to dominate the system of election administration. Nonetheless, for sake of simplicity and to avoid re-labeling the plan's long standing emphasis of it, this consideration of it will generally use the shortened title.

The direct election plan which emerged for full Senate consideration in the summer of 1979 would eliminate the allocation of electoral votes now based in the federal design since there would be no electoral votes at all. The states, as states, would not be a factor in determining the outcome of the election as is presently the case. Presumably some national office would be used or established for the purpose of reporting the count either from each precinct or via some state canvassing agency.

Although the direct vote plan does not include or refer to the nominating process and only the actual election, it will be shown later that full nationalization of the nominating and election process is a most likely prospect. Such enactments by the Congress would have a substantial impact on the prevailing nominating arrangements in the states and could eliminate them entirely.

Proponents of the plan make no pretense of hiding the prospect that a candidate would be elected who did not receive a majority of the total of popular votes. Indeed, the very design of the plan would encourage that prospect. Only a plurality of the total vote would be needed to insure election, if that plurality reached as much as 40 percent of the total.

Advocates of the plan have not been fully united on the need for a contingency feature or, indeed, of the style of any contingency arrangement. There seems to be complete unity that any contingency arrangement would not mean a decision by the Congress. But

66

although the proposal defeated in the Senate in 1979 contained a contingency feature, it appears to have been included because of the prospect that several candidates would so divide the national vote that the plurality would (or could) be quite low, even less than 25 percent. Thus, fearing that possibility, proponents of direct election joined in the scheme for a runoff of the two top vote-getters as nationally tabulated if no candidate received as much as 40 percent of the vote.

In sum, the direct vote plan can be described as a national plebicite, with as many candidates in the field as supporters can muster, presuming no tightening of requirements for having a place on the ballot. The winner would not have to have a majority of the vote. Only if the contingency were required would there be a "majority" president.

The direct vote plan suggests numerous collateral issues and these will be considered in the pages which follow. Additional consideration will be given in a later chapter as the issues about it narrow.

As proponents of the plan describe it, the plan is one of ultimate and obvious simplicity, easily understood, wholly democratic with every vote equal to any other, and one which would end the advantages or disadvantages of the electoral college system to any bloc, group, region, political party or state.

The plan is characterized by supporters as one which also is comprehensive and its completeness thereby overshadows all other plans. Longley and Braun state that it is the only plan which deals fully with "all five of the problems of the contemporary electoral college system."[2] To them, those problems are the abolishing of the electoral college "in all respects" and thereby eliminating the problem of defecting electors, state equality through the "constant two" electoral votes, the general-ticket system, the contingency feature for possible election in the House, and "selection reversal possibilities." Opponents of the plan do not completely dispute that it does address them, but they quickly point out that election by a direct national vote would raise problems greater than the cure is intended to provide.

The most frequently voiced argument in favor of the plan is that it embraces the most essential characteristics of a democracy: it is designed to ensure

that there be absolute equal voting power by all
voters regardless of location or status. Proponents
urge that it is in harmony with the current period in
history which places strong emphasis on human rights
and individual equality. Advocates also insist that
the plan is the only one which would ensure that the
candidate elected would have a broad and unquestioned
mandate to govern successfully.

Supporters of direct election insist that it would
end disputes about who won and who lost and especially
would end post-election "deals" by electors or by
members of the House. Thus, there would be an early
decision in November and the winning candidate would
assume his duties on schedule. This assumes no runoff was necessary, however.

Proponents insist that the plan would preserve
and invigorate the political party system, especially
the two-party arrangement. Under the plan, one-party
states would cease to exist or be vastly reduced in
their significance. Two-party competition would be
enhanced. At the same time, and to ensure that all
political persuasions were permitted, third or minor
parties would be encouraged or more inclined to emerge.
The result would be to vastly increase voter interest
and turnout since voters everywhere would know that
their vote "counted" and could not be "transferred"
to another candidate or "taken away." Furthermore,
each vote would be "direct" and the result would not
come about, as is presently done, from an indirect
system which is an accumulation of majorities and
pluralities after ultimate action by the presidential
electors.

Concerns about fraud in elections has long been
prevalent especially in close elections. Advocates of
direct election maintain that no longer would there be
the prospect that the person elected was so annointed
because of false returns however arrived at. No
longer would there need to be much interest in "what
might have happened" if a few hundred votes or even
a few thousand votes in this or that state had been
cast differently or were counted as a result of fraud
or other error. There would be no needless delay in
knowing the results on election night.

One strong advocate of direct election, Neal
Peirce, sums up the case for it by emphasizing that
there would be an end to the disenfranchisement of
voters who vote for the loser since each vote would

become a part of the national total for each candidate and tallied accordingly.[3] This is a central point expressed in most debates favoring the direct election plan.

In his "Direct Election of the President," Zeidenstein advances the direct vote plan by route of analyzing real and alleged defects in all other plans. His criteria for an election arrangement have been presented, but as with the advocacy by Longley and Braun, Zeidenstein finds that only the direct vote plan meets the essentials and in their entirety. His work is severely critical of arguments of others who question the plan's propriety and is especially harsh about the views of major spokesmen who would favor continuing the present electoral college system.[4]

A more measured approach to the issues about the direct vote is by Sindler.[5] He observes that of the several proposals, the direct vote plan "is the most radical of the reform options, displacing EC [electoral college] root and branch." He states that the plan "provides for literal vote equality" and thereby deprives pivotal populous states and their "organized interest groups" of special advantages presently enjoyed, but also that they would "still remain influential because of sheer numbers of voters." This is a recognition of the nationalization feature of the direct vote. But some critics suggest that it would reduce the power of Black voters in the more populous states such as New York and Illinois. This reaction is countered with a claim that even if it occurred, the strength loss would be compensated for with votes in the South and some other northern states.

Sindler addresses the issue about gains and losses and advantages of blocs or organized interests among population concentrations stating that the direct vote congressional managers ". . . walked a fine line between assuring populous states of high influence [under it] in spite of the end of the EC's state-unit rule and assuring small states of increased influence. . ."

In considering the 40 percent vote requirement as a minimum to win, Sindler says there is "nothing sacrosanct and little proved about the 40 percent figure. . ." He notes that lower or higher figures were suggested in the hearings and debates. The 40 percent figures seems to have origins in a recognition that a majority would be unlikely of all votes cast

69

and a plurality would generally prevail with 60 percent divided among all other candidates and the bulk
of that proportion going to the candidate of the other
major party. Usually cited is the vote realized by
Abraham Lincoln in 1860 with just under 40 percent of
the total. Promoters of the direct vote apparently do
not want a majority decision since to have it a runoff would be likely much of the time.

The issue about the size of the vote needed includes the factor of "legitimacy" and a president ought
to have, indeed, must have a strong popular mandate to
govern. This belief gave rise to suggestions that the
minimum percentage should be no less than 45 percent
since in recent times only Woodrow Wilson in 1912 and
Nixon in 1968 had not realized that figure. Others
thought that the anticipated increase in party competition and the prospects of several strong party candidates would mean frequent runoff elections if the minimum were too high and the lower figure of 40 percent
gained general support among proponents. It is an
obvious compromise between a few supporters of a
suggested 35 percent and the higher 45 percent. The
40 percent was contained in the House approved proposal in 1969 and in the Senate version defeated in
1979.

The debate about the needed plurality and acceptance of the 40 percent requirement made a contingency
feature a virtual necessity. Not all proponents of
direct vote, however, would agree. To some, a plurality vote of whatever magnitude is all that should be
required. But most backers of direct vote insist on a
contingency feature and the runoff is widely favored.
Whereas other plans have included action by the House
or in a joint session, direct vote adherents reject
any congressional feature. To do so would violate
the idea of a "people's president." At one time, however, Senator Bayh supported a contingency plan in the
congress over a popular runoff or indicated it would
be an acceptable alternative.

Under the direct vote plan a contingency feature
assumes that there will be three or more candidates
and political parties. But proponents found themselves in the awkward position of advocating party
competition as an essential element of democracy and
then were faced with having a president with a low
plurality vote. Some direct vote supporters suggested
that perhaps the electoral college vote should be used
if the required plurality percentage was not realized

in total popular vote, such as the 40 percent. This suggestion did not gain much favor especially among the egalitarians who disavow any use of the electoral college system of allocating votes. This was one element in the so-called "federal plan" presented earlier. Sindler stated that had the Senate voted on the measure in 1969 or 1970 the runoff feature would not have been retained.

Sayre and Parris[6] open their analysis of the direct vote plan with this observation: "While the idea of the direct-vote plan is simple, its implications are complex and uncertain. The President would be elected with a very different mandate than he has today." To them, (the plan would mean that the most populous states would lose a "great strategic importance.") Blocs of votes would be less likely "delivered." This would mean, as others have indicated, a shift of the relative power of some states or the states generally. (A candidate would devote much of his time where it might be expected he could gain a large plurality of votes to overcome a possible narrow division in strongly competitive two-party states.) With the prospective lessening of the influence of major population states or areas, and the leverage on public policy which has often resulted, new forces would come into dominance or their influence would be greater. How would this change affect ethnic interests? Would the result mean a sharpening of competing interests in domestic programs challenged by small town and more rural regions? Would some suburban areas sometimes outvoted because of larger and more unified blocs of core-city voters gain in influence and more nearly dominate policy which is of deep concern to core-city residents? Sayre and Parris also observe that in this process the impact results or may result from the different way the election is determined: under the direct plan the base line is away from representative voting, that is, through the presidential electors, to a nationwide tally. One is of total votes cast, the other is the result of votes cast for about 80 percent of the electoral votes--at least from population distribution.

These writers believe the direct vote plan would significantly alter the very nature of the political party system with its greatest impact on "the number and the internal power structure of the parties." There seems to be little disagreement with the observation that third parties would increase in numbers. But Sayre and Parris suggest that a combination of third parties might prevent one candidate from reaching the required 40 percent plurality and the runoff would be necessary. "In sum, the runoff provision of the direct-vote amendment would raise the expectations and almost certainly increase the incentives of minor parties to enter the presidential race and perhaps eventually to enter state and local contests." The possible impact on the two major parties would be obvious.

What kind of a campaign would be waged in a runoff? Would the victor between the two running result in a victory for the candidate most preferred in the first race? Or, would the final selection be the second choice of most voters or even one they strongly opposed?

Objections to contingency plans generally center on the desire to prevent "deals" and "bargaining." The runoff would not prevent them. Which is the lesser of the possible evils, a runoff or no runoff and in the latter the prospect that the plurality winner might have a low proportion of the total popular vote.

Bargaining and compromises are commonplace in nominating conventions. Would similar conditions prevail in a runoff election? A nominating convention ultimately supports a single presidential candidate, or does most of the time. Any bargaining is intended to gain maximum party support. In a runoff, however, the contest would be between two different party candidates who presumably would have to seek support from followers of other candidates or the other candidates themselves. Would there be agreements between the two top contenders in a runoff to limit the issues to be discussed? What would be the role of the state and local party organizations in a runoff? Is it practical to assume that party leaders could mount an aggressive second election campaign?

The 40 percent feature does not guarantee that the top vote getter would have a majority vote, but if the 40 percent was not realized then the runoff feature would be used. The runoff would produce a majority winner, and it is not easy to reconcile the contrast. It would seem that democratic purists would insist upon majority rule.

Views vary extensively about the effects of the direct vote plan upon the political party system and

especially on the two-party tradition. Sayre and
Parris believe the two major parties would become more
homogenous. Presumably dissidents, those too uncom-
fortable in one of the major parties would go elsewhere or form a new party. Would these prospects mean
regional parties? Ideological? Economic? Some
wholly issue oriented? Would state party organizations
be strengthened or split apart? Would a prospective
increase in the number and strength and disparity of
political parties lessen the importance of the party
in presidential politics? How would this affect
state and local campaigns and elections?

In considering the pros and cons about the direct
vote plan little attention is ordinarily given to the
nominating process, but the impact of the plan on the
process cannot be overlooked. Sayre and Parris believe there would be less inclination of the parties
to select candidates from large states. Greater re-
liance would be put on a candidate's ability to use
national television effectively, but that is a major
factor presently. In contest, undoubedly, would be
the existing system of presidential primaries and
the caucus system of selecting delegates. And whatever
the tie between delegate support from a given state
or area and ultimate voter support from the same
entities one would agree with Sayre and Parris that
under the direct vote plan the so-called "safe states"
would be "done."

Money in elections has long been an issue whether
in presidential politics or otherwise. Some major
control over contributions and the use of money in
elections is now public policy, albeit not fully
refined, and provision has been made for public funds
in presidential campaigns. If the direct vote plan is
adopted and the runoff feature is included, what provisions would be made to finance it? The time would
be short to obtain commitments from non-public sources.
Would the runoff be thereby financed entirely or nearly
so from public funds? Undoubtedly much of the financing emphasis on television in campaigns may be of
growing concern regardless of the system used for
electing the president.

Few references are made in the discourse about a
runoff of its effect on the candidates physically and
psychologically. Even the most vigorous would find it
a challenge of substance. It is another argument
against the use of a runoff.

Advocates of the direct vote plan usually address voter turnout. Voter turnout in the United States is distressingly low. Would the expected competition for the national popular vote make voters more sensitive and aware of the place of their vote on the outcome? With the chant that every vote would count, would the direct vote thereby prod otherwise indifferent eligible voters to change their ways and vote? Sayre and Parris state that the "potential benefits in civic education is considerable." One would readily agree.

The analysis of the direct vote by Sayre and Parris include other matters. They express concern about the impact of direct election on the office of president. Although using past election data is speculative, they believe that the prospect of having close popular elections is problematical. This might be true most of the time, but the 1960 and 1968 and 1976 elections could hardly be considered landslides!

Would a close election in the direct vote plan weaken the presidency any more than those close elections considering only the total popular vote? Would a runoff produce a close vote or would it make the prospect less likely? There may be no election plan which would prevent close vote results, although the national bonus plan contains some elements of one.

Even though it is hazardous to predict the prospective actions of voters, advocates of direct election highlight the feature that all votes are "counted." And the sequel is that the prospects are excellent that there will be a plurality winner most of the time. But under the 40 percent rule and a narrow division between the two top candidates, would there not be the possibility that as at present the shift of a few thousand votes could change the outcome? Under that feature the mandate to govern might be weaker than under the electoral college system where as least a majority vote is ultimately obtained.

In considering the runoff feature and possible problems in its use there is some experience in several of the states for state offices. Some value might come from an examination of the use of runoffs such as in France.

Of some concern to those believing in continuation of at least some elements of the federal system even in the selection of a president is that under the direct election plan it would not be long until the entire system for electing the president would be nationalized. Would the authority now vested in the states be pre-empted by the Congress as a by-product of the direct vote plan? Would the prevailing diversity among the states in even minor detail be cast aside in favor of strict national uniformity? Any enumeration of items involved would be lengthy, but the identification of the most familiar will suffice to indicate what might be involved.

One guide to the intent of advocates of direct election is the specifics contained in S. J. 28, the 1979 proposal, and the accompanying analysis of the amendment. (These are included in the Appendix).

Chief among the nationalization elements are those which would give the Congress authority to prescribe uniform national residence requirements and thereby affect also registration of voters. If done, same-day registration (election day), postal card registration, or other "instant" styles of voter registration could be imposed on the states. Lengthy residence requirements should not prevail under any circumstances, but it is not a very persuasive argument to insist that a few days, even thirty days, of residency would unduly restrict the franchise. The assumption is often advanced that residency requirements are designed to prevent some individuals or groups in some particular categories from voting. The result may be just that, but more positive reasons can be couched in an earnest desire to promote voter knowledge (or better insure it) and understanding of state and local issues and candidates. The alternative would be for the states to hold separate elections for the president and vice-president and on a different day for all other candidates, or if on the same day to screen all voters if the different residency requirements were not met for both sets of candidates. This would be a formidable activity in each polling place and with that prospect the states would probably succumb to the national prescription.

A second possible nationalization feature in the proposed amendment is in the section authorizing the Congress to alter the "times, places, and manner" of holding the election, including the proposed runoff. For the Congress to establish a single day for the election would not alter present practice. The original Constitutional provision authorized the Congress to fix the time and the day, the latter to be uniform throughout the United States--these being for the election of the electoral college electors.

The language of S. J. 28, however, would extend the power of the Congress so that the hours of voting, for example, and the specifications for polling places could be determined by national mandate. Furthermore, the "manner" of holding elections is readily interpreted to include the selection of election administrators, polling clerks, and judges. Would national rules also be prescribed covering party workers and other "unofficial" workers, such as "watchers" and challengers? Having two sets of regulations, one for state and local balloting and another for national offices, would seem most improbable. State compliance with national rules for all elections would be the likely prospect.

Another clause would grant authority to the Congress to determine who would be included on the ballot for president. Although the experience in 1968 and 1980, for example, illustrate efforts to deny a place on the ballot for Wallace and Anderson respectively, the pattern may well be set that these efforts would rarely if ever be repeated for major contenders. The analysis accompanying S. J. 28 states that "if a State sought to exclude a major party candidate from appearing on the ballot. . . the Congress would be empowered to deal with such a situation." Presumably implicit in the authority granted is that the Congress would define what constitutes a major political party. Would it not follow that it would also define what constitutes a political party?

The proposed amendment requires that the results of the regular election in November be declared no later than thirty days after that election. This is a highly desirable feature, but seems predicated on the likelihood that runoffs would be frequent, otherwise why thirty days? The electoral college electors meet about mid-December (the first Monday after the second Wednesday) and their vote is forwarded to Washington, D. C. to be received by the Congress after it convenes in January.

The time available following the election now is about six weeks before the electoral vote is cast. The thirty day rule presumably is considered adequate for counting and any recounting, but is it adequate for challenges? With current widespread diversity among the states on these factors would probably bring a set of national standards into being including a likely shift of jurisdiction from state to U.S. courts.

The proposed amendment does not contain a time-table for a runoff. The Congress is authorized to deal with it. If the regular election results were certified no earlier than the thirty-day deadline, the runoff schedule would be extremely tight. The latter could not take place until early December at the earliest. The Congress could stipulate alternative dates, one earlier if the results were certified shortly after the election, and a later one if they were not certified until the deadline. Except in close elections the two top contenders to enter a runoff would be known well in advance of the certification and a second campaign could be under way quickly. Nonetheless, the time remaining after a runoff election for the counting, recounts, and challenges is narrow.

The language of the proposed amendment does not affect the provisions of the 20th Amendment requiring the new president to take his oath on January 20 after the November election. If this were to be strictly observed, then congressional action would need to be taken to constrain the time alloted for all post-election activity and possibly the basis for challenges and the adjudication of them.

Regardless of the extent of possible nationalization under the direct vote proposal, the Nation is not without some experience in such a development. Notable is the system of authorizing national regis-trars and surveillance by the U.S. Attorney General in elections, including state and local, resulting from provisions of the voting rights acts of the Congress. The procedures applicable are based upon particularized situations, but the precedent is set for expanding the use of national officers into all election administration. Furthermore, also already in operation is the Federal Election Commission estab-lished by the Congress in 1974 relating primarily to campaign financing. It could be a short step to ex-pand the Commission's authority into all phases of election administration. If this were done would an incumbent national administration be tempted to manip-ulate the outcome as Sayre and Parris suggest?

Peirce and Longley address the issue about the desirability of the direct vote plan with a chapter

77

ed "Today's Alternative: Direct Vote or the Quo." To them any of the other alternatives nted over the years do not erase defects of the e. toral college and state that "either the country will continue with the existing electoral college [7] system or it will shift to a direct popular vote." Their argument for an "either or" situation is centered around what they consider are the basic issues. These are the "concurrent majority," the place of the two-party system, the impact of the direct vote on the federal system, and questions about pluralities, majorities, and runoffs. They observe that "the runoff does pose some problems"[8] which is a reflection that the supporters of the direct vote plan are not unified on the need for that kind of contin-gency or none at all.

They conclude their thesis in this way: "No one has been able to show how the preservation of a quaint eighteenth-century voting device, the electoral college, with all its anomalies and potential wild cards, can serve to protect the Republic. The choice of the chief executive must be the people's, and it should rest with none other than them."[9]

The next chapter reviews the activity in the Congress leading to the 1979 Senate vote on the direct national popular vote proposal.

FOOTNOTES

1. <u>Op</u>. <u>cit</u>., p. 113.

2. <u>Op</u>. <u>cit</u>., p. 82.

3. 1977 Senate <u>Hearings</u>, pp. 247-251. In a 1981
   revision of Peirce's <u>The People's President</u>,
   he and Lawrence D. Longley update and extend the
   endorsement of electing the president by a direct
   national popular vote.

4. <u>Op</u>. <u>cit</u>.

5. <u>Op</u>. <u>cit</u>.

6. <u>Op</u>. <u>cit</u>., Ch. IV.

7. Peirce, Neal R., and Lawrence D. Longley, <u>The
   People's President - The Electoral College in
   American History and the Direct Vote Alternative</u>,
   (New Haven: Yale University Press, 1981, revised
   edition), p. 207.

8. <u>Ibid</u>., p. 221.

9. <u>Ibid</u>., p. 236.

Chapter VII. The Hearings and Debates

Early in the First Session of the 91st Congress
in 1969 more than fifty proposals to change the method
of electing the president were introduced in the House.
The high number is some evidence of the concerns at
the time that the recently concluded election in 1968
might have turned out quite differently. Such speculation gave encouragement to supporters of change that
1969 was the year to abolish the electoral college
and to substitute, many hoped, a direct national popular election plan. Many of the proposals were exact
duplicates, but among the total were most of the recently advocated alternatives.

The leadership of the House Committee on the
Judiciary determined that these measures should be
the subject of public hearings early in the session
and beginning on February 5 and continuing periodically
to March 13 ten days of hearings were held before the
full committee. The tone of the hearings was set by
the chairman, Emanuel Celler, Democrat of New York.[1]

Today the Committee on the Judiciary begins
several days of public hearings on proposals to
amend the Constitution to revise the method by
which we elect our Chief Executive. These proposals raise issues fundamental to our political
system and call for a review of constitutional
provisions which guide this Nation as a Federal
Union. They also affect the maintenance of the
two party system which has served this Nation
well.

Proponents of change have a substantial
burden. The existing system is familiar and until
recent years has not prompted widespread outcries
for reform. However, several elections, and
especially the most recent presidential election
[1968], underscore a potential instability in
the existing procedures.

The possibility of deadlock and vacancy of
uncertain duration in the principal office of this
Government poses a substantial danger that many
Americans, regardless of region or party, agree
must be eliminated.

The chairman also expressed the view that presidential electors might not observe the dictates of the voters as a few had done and that the voters had to rely on the states to operate the system. Those views were reflected in Celler's own proposals and also in several others to be considered by the committee. Some sixty individuals appeared before the committee to give testimony and responded to questions or comments from committee members. Approximately two-thirds of the presentations were by members of the House, many of whom were sponsors of proposals under review. Some were also members of the committee who also had introduced one or more resolutions. Additionally, twenty-five members of the House sent letters or statements advocating one or more of the changes presented, or conversely opposing any change or indicating support for only minor changes in the electoral process.

Twenty-four states were represented in the testimony from House members and these were from the smallest to the most populous and ranged from all parts of the Nation.

Others testifying included representatives from such diverse groups as the American Bar Association, the U.S. Chamber of Commerce, the Liberty Lobby, the American Farm Bureau, the AFL-CIO, the American Good Government Society, the National Cotton Council, the NAACP, the ILGWU, the American Jewish Congress, members of the academic community, and spokesmen for some organizations often conducting election research. Positions taken by these groups will be reflected in the analysis of Senate action on similar proposals later in this chapter.

The testimony and the statements or other communications cover over 1,000 pages. The resolutions alone comprise more than three hundred of these printed pages. The testimony and communications, as a whole, reflect detailed consideration of the issues about the electoral college system and the several alternatives which had been under consideration or discussion for many years. Some were covered in more detail than others, but the hearings served that purpose well. Approximately twenty-seven hours were devoted to them during the ten day period.

Public review of proposals before legislative bodies is a hallmark of a democratic society. Open sessions are considered not only essential, but mandatory on proposals to change the Constitution. Views vary, however, about the actual usefulness of hearings. As one writer put it, "it is in the committee room that the Congressman spends a good deal of his time, and there the real legislative work is done."[2] There are exceptions, to be sure, but it is in committees and subcommittees that a detailed study of proposals can be made and where interested individuals may be given the opportunity to present their views about them in public hearings.

On the other hand, the more cynical critic may insist that hearings are largely matters of scenery to satisfy the public and are so regarded by many members of the Congress who conduct them.

Generally, however, committees and their subcommittees are referred to as the "little legislatures" and vital to the process. Their use extends to a wide spectrum of the entire activity of the Congress and provides it with a vehicle and forum to participate more effectively in the powers the Congress shares with the other branches of the government.

Depending upon the assumed importance of a proposal at the time, it may be considered first by the full committee having jurisdiction. But usually hearings are first undertaken by a subcommittee having cognizance of the subject matter involved. The resulting deliberations are reported and then reviewed by the full parent committee for a decision.

Views about the place of the subcommittee, committee, and hearings process vary among observers. They may not always agree on the influence of the entire process on the success or failure of a measure, but they generally agree that there would be a marked void if the hearings were not a part of it and especially the public nature of them. This is especially true in any review of proposals to amend the Constitution.

One review of the committee system and hearings emphasized that the hearings "serve to extend and expose the committee role systems." They also "can be considered a focal point for consensus development in the political system. In a nation with such marked social, economic, cultural, and political heterogeneities there is need for several stages of consensus development before ideas are transformed into policies. Public committee hearings are valuable in this respect."[3]

In his Governmental Process, David Truman out-
lines the purposes and functions of congressional
committee hearings.[4]

> First, the hearing is a means of trans-
> mitting information, both technical and politi-
> cal, from various actual and potential interest
> groups to the committee. This is the most
> familiar function, and probably the least im-
> portant. From the standpoint of the interest
> group or the committee member, . . . the hearing
> is usually a haphazard and unsatisfactory device
> for giving and receiving information. This is
> one function of such proceedings, but it alone
> would not account for their continued vitality.
> A second use is as a propaganda channel through
> which a public may be extended and its segments
> partially consolidated or reinforced. A third
> function is to provide a quasi-ritualistic means
> of adjusting group conflicts and relieving dis-
> turbances through a safety valve.

A former member of the House from California,
Clem Miller, wrote of his experiences and views about
the hearings process.[5]

> Congressional hearings serve many purposes.
> The principal one is to build the recorded base
> of knowledge upon which legislation can be con-
> structed. Even where there is the honest desire
> of the committee, its crabbed way must seem
> strange to the untutored bystander. Many of the
> issues before Congress have been around for years.
> The chairman may be excused if he leaves holes in
> his investigation. Why develop a long line of
> inquiry when it was fully covered by Report umpty-
> ump of the 84th Congress?

> Many times, the hearings seem to be pro
> forma, just going through the motions, with the key
> decisions already made. They resemble a large
> verbal orchestration, as a "record" is carefully
> shaped under the vigilant gavel of the chairman.
> A standard parade of witnesses files by from the
> national organizations--AF of L, U.S. Chamber of
> Commerce, National Association of Manufacturers--
> then a seasoning of university professors, and so
> on. The witnesses are carved up or blown up, or

tailored to the need. Some are dismissed peremp-
torily, others are drawn out solicitously.

A sometime staff member to then Senator Lyndon B.
Johnson wrote of the hearings process by focusing attention on the objectives of a committee member.

He may wish to make himself a national leader,
built a reputation as a subject-matter expert, ad-
vertise himself to his constituency, do a favor for
a supporter, discharge some of his own aggression--
the list could be a long one. What is important is
to see that in every aspect of congressional life
it is necessary to satisfy both the system needs
and the largely personal needs of the member who
must keep himself solvent in a free-enterprise
politics.[6]

The role of members of the Congress assigned the
task of public hearings varies widely. Anyone who has
attended hearings will readily recognize that, as a
whole, they are not impartial and unbiased arbiters
about the matters being considered. They do take
sides. As one writer put it:

This is not difficult to understand if we
remember the conditions under which legislators
are appointed to committees and the norms to which
many of them respond once appointed. In both cases
the legislator's background, interest, and constituency pressures contribute to making him much
less than an impartial judge of facts. He would
not be a member of Congress unless he willingly
accepted political struggle as a perpetual fact
of his every day life.[7]

Traditionally, a subcommittee is under substantial
influence of its chairman and especially respecting
the general management of committee activities. Significant are such matters as when hearings are to be held,
how much time will be allocated to them, who should be
invited to testify--there is no "right" to testify--
the general order of the testimony, the questioning of
witnesses, and generally, handling the decorum of the
sessions.

Frequently a subcommittee hearing is virtually a
one-man show with only the chairman presiding and par-
ticipating, or it may include other members all of the
time or some of the time especially when a particular
interest group is testifying or a constituent is offer-

ing views. If the chairman is already known to favor a proposal under review he may or may not have more than a parochial interest and his position even as chairman may be openly that of an avowed proponent. On occasion, of course, he may assume the role also of an expert.

The roles of a chairman and other members will differ with changing subject matter. This was quite evident in the House hearings in 1969 on proposals to change the method of electing the president and even more pronounced in the companion Senate hearings that year and the decade following. Alignments on these proposals were not according to strict political party associations.

A subcommittee (or committee) chairman relies heavily on the professional staff assigned. With specialization dominant in the hearings and review process the staff members are chosen in large part because of their individual expertise or their capacity to develop it. Some staff members have been associated with a particular subcommittee or committee for several years, but the turnover may be heavy when chairmen change, or there are infusions of new members, or when the party majority changes.

There are practical limits on the amount of time a committee or subcommittee can devote to public sessions on any particular measure before them. To have all members attend all sessions may be highly desirable, but the record shows that they do not and some of them rarely do. Some do not attend at all. Proposals for constitutional change may be in a somewhat different category and should require greater effort and more sustained interest than many legislative proposals. The extent to which this prevails will vary with proposals as much as with the views or stand of individual members.

A significant feature of the hearing process is that it is done publicly and the result made available. There are some exceptions, or course, with off-the-record discussions and executive sessions. The published hearings may be voluminous. For many hearings few individuals from the general public attend and not alone due to limitations of space. The printed record, though accessible, is read by few also. The results may often show too little planning, poor organization, and evidence of bias by committee members, although this is expected by those testifying, at least for some of them. The hearings usually show, however, that on the whole there was consideration of the major issues, albeit at times most unevenly.

At the conclusion of the House committee hearings in 1969, they were printed and a report prepared. Generally hearings carry the label "Printed for the use of the Committee on . . ." but additional copies are provided for wider distribution. Perhaps because of the interest in the proposals for changing the method of electing the president, the Report of the Committee on the Judiciary of fifty-two pages was offered for sale through the Superintendent of Documents at a price of twenty-five cents.[8]

The Committee recommended approval of the proposal for the direct national popular election of the president on April 29, 1969 by a vote of twenty-nine to six. Three Democrats and three Republicans opposed it. There were twenty Democrats and fifteen Republicans on the Committee at the time.

As is not uncommon, the Report carried the majority position and analysis, and additionally the views of the minority. Two minority positions were included. One of them concluded that "no convincing demonstration has been offered in either the course of the committee hearings or in the majority report to rationalize a 40-percent plurality requirement." And the other, "After weeks of testimony reviewing extensively the history of presidential elections, it must be concluded that our committee has overreacted to this problem."

The mood of the House membership at this stage was for approval of the proposal and the House leadership responded by placing a high priority for early debate and House vote. The Committee Report was available in May, 1969, and on September 18 the matter was before the full House. After a futile attempt to recommit it back to the Committee with instructions to incorporate the district plan, which was defeated by a vote of 246 to 162, the measure was then approved by the House by a vote of 338 to 70. Of the seventy, twenty-six were Republicans and forty-four Democrats. All but three of the latter were from southern states.[9]

Soon after the House action, on September 30, President Nixon endorsed the proposal. "Because the ultimate goal of electoral reform must prevail over differences as to how best to achieve that goal, I endorse the direct election approach and urge the Senate also to adopt it."[10]

The route to an ultimate vote in the Senate was long and troubled. It was as colorful on occasion as it was prolonged and frequently boring with repetitive appearances and presentations. The hearings process lasted into 1979, intermittently. Although the House acted promptly following the availability of the hearings and published report, the Senate did not vote until the summer of 1979. No further action was taken by the House after the 1969 favorable decision.

Since consideration by the Senate was extensive and recent, especial attention will be given to the Senate role. And as might be assumed those testifying before the House Committee on the Judiciary and organizational views given were largely the same as before the Senate subcommittee or committee, reference will be made to the Senate side in this analysis. The Senate membership changed during the 1970s with numerous new ones and these changes were also reflected in committee assignments. Generally, the issue before the subcommittee or committee was to be almost wholly one of favoring the direct election plan or retaining the electoral college. Other proposals which had been reviewed in the early stages gradually fell by the wayside.

The Subcommittee on Constitutional Amendments of the Senate Committee on the Judiciary commenced hearings on January 23, 1969, a few days before the House Committee began its deliberations. The Senate hearings continued from time to time until May 2 of that year and were scheduled during a period of eleven days.[11] In printed form, the testimony, discussion, statements and the like comprise 620 pages. Additionally, there is included an appendix of more than 400 pages. The record shows that a span of more than twenty-five hours was devoted to the hearings, but there were interruptions and recesses which shortened the actual time involved.

The Subcommittee was chaired by Senator Birch Bayh, Democrat of Indiana. As did his counterpart holding the House hearings, he favored the direct vote plan.

Sixteen members of the House and Senate presented their views. Some twenty other individuals also gave testimony. Some state government officials testified. Organizations having representatives who testified had also appeared before the House committee or were scheduled to do so. Favoring the direct vote, or generally favoring it with some minor changes, included the

88

American Bar Association, the AFL-CIO, the ILGWU, the Civil Liberties Union, the Americans for Democratic Action, a group called the Let Us Vote Campaign, and the National Small Business Association. Opposing, but not necessarily endorsing the electoral college system, were such groups as the American Farm Bureau, the National Cotton Council, the American Jewish Congress, and the American Good Government Society, Inc. Members of the academic community were divided as were representatives of organizations often conducting election research.

Attorney General John N. Mitchell made a presentation before the House committee, but he did not appear before the Senate group. In the House process he endorsed the direct vote with some modifications, for the Senate hearing a deputy attorney general appeared to extend approval of the direct vote plan.

It will be recalled that at the time of the casting of the vote in the electoral college in December 1968 there was one "faithless elector" in North Carolina, Dr. Lloyd Bailey, who cast his vote for George Wallace rather than Nixon who had the plurality of the vote in the state. Dr. Bailey's observations have already been presented.

Of those testifying before the Senate subcommittee, only five were opposed to the direct vote plan and virtually all of the others either favored it or favored it with some reservations. This line-up was in sharp contrast to the House hearings, at least in numbers. This tally of numbers who appeared before the subcommittee does not reflect the presentations by members of the House and Senate who testified. Some control is exercised over those appearing from the "outside" but prevailing courtesy dictates that a member of the Congress has a virtual "right" to appear. A member may be persuaded, if necessary, to be brief!

The early action by the Committee on the Judiciary and the subcommittee to hold hearings in January may have adversely affected the ability of the minority--those opposed to the direct vote plan--to select and arrange for witnesses. But this may not be a wholly valid observation since the hearings continued into the month of May. In any event, whether balanced or not by numbers and talent, the essential arguments pro and con were presented.

After the hearings were concluded the subcommittee recommended approval of the direct vote plan. But no further action was taken in 1969 and more hearings were held early the following year.

Reactions from opponents of the direct vote plan may have been strong enough to prompt the 1970 hearings being undertaken by the full committee rather than the subcommittee. It may have been the result of the small number opposing it who were invited or permitted to testify in 1969. Opinions of those involved vary. It may have been the persuasive influence of the Committee chairman, Senator James O. Eastland, Democrat of Mississippi and Committee member, Senator Sam J. Ervin, Jr., Democrat of North Carolina, both opponents of direct vote. In any event, three days were given to the hearings with Senator Ervin serving as acting chairman.

The timing and other arrangements for the hearings brought a strong reaction from Senator Bayh.[12]

> ". . . I want the record to show . . . concern, about the manner in which these hearings have been organized. It gives credence to the fact that these hearings were called not to have the opportunity to share the thoughts of many expert witnesses and to have a thorough study of this problem, but indeed as an effort to defeat direct election.

> I say, with all due respect to the acting chairman, that even his statement, instead of spending the time that he used to support his position, was mostly an effort to destroy the credibility of direct election.

> . . . I think the record will show that the way these hearings have been organized, not the fact that we are having them but the way they have been organized, is the most blatant disregard for senatorial courtesy I have experienced in 8 years in the Senate.

> As the subcommittee chairman, I was not consulted as to the dates these hearings were to be held. I was in no way consulted on the witness list that we were to hear. I found out only by accident late Friday evening, when a staff member of mine had a gratuitous phone call from another staff member, only by accident that we were going

to have the hearings on this date.

And when we found the initial witness list, much to our surprise and consternation, and no fault of the witnesses involved, all 10 witnesses then invited to come and listed as witnesses were antidirect election witnesses. At my insistence, then, Monday morning the League of Women Voters was added as the last witness on the Friday schedule. At my further insistence, the American Bar Association was added and the Chamber of Commerce was added.

In his response, Senator Ervin supported the action to begin the hearings on April 15 since there was to be a committee vote on the proposal for direct election on April 24. He further stated that "an agreement" had been reached to take that vote. Thus, the only surprise for Senator Bayh was the schedule for the hearings, not that a vote would be taken by the Committee membership. Senator Ervin further noted that he as "chairman" [acting chairman] was exercising his rights and "did just exactly what any committee chairman has the right to do and power to do." He said he felt there ought to be some hearings and so they were scheduled "for this week."

This interchange probably did not alter the views of the members of the Committee, eight of whom were present for the first day of hearings, but it demonstrates some of the sharp differences on the issues and some commentary about committee operations.

The 1970 hearings comprise over 270 printed pages with an appendix of an additional 100 pages. Twenty-three individuals appeared to present views in the course of the three days. Five were members of the Congress. The record shows that a span of approximately fourteen hours was devoted to the hearings, but the schedule was laced with some interruptions and recesses.

Repeating their earlier positions favoring direct election were representatives of the Chamber of Commerce, the American Bar Association, and the League of Women Voters. Appearing in opposition were members of the academic community, representatives of the National Secretaries of State, and made more colorful by the testimony of Theodore H. White, noted author and political analyst.

91

Notwithstanding the allegation of bias in the scheduling and in witness selection, the issues were again stated and argued. Committee members actively participated in the discussion and indeed more may have been gained, if only for the record, with proponents of direct vote on the Committee pitted against opponents of the plan. Having concluded the hearings on April 17, the Committee on the Judiciary voted a week later to report the proposal to the full Senate.[14] The Committee Report was not available until August, however.[15]

Supporters of the proposal reportedly had commitments favoring it from fifty-eight Senators, or nine votes short of the maximum number needed if all Senators voted. Debate commenced on September 8, 1970 and continued intermittently into October. The debate bore all of the marks by opponents of a filibuster and a cloture petition was introduced and considered on September 17. The vote on cloture was taken and was six votes short of the needed number. Debate resumed and another cloture petition was filed and considered on September 29, but again was short of the required number, being fifty-three to thirty-four.

Debate again was resumed and floor discussion indicates that a third cloture petition effort would be undertaken, but agreement was reached that the matter should be delayed until the following month.[16] However, no further action was taken by the Senate that year.

The issue was somewhat dormant the next two years with no formal consideration until the Subcommittee on Constitutional Amendments scheduled more hearings in late September 1973. Only two days were given to them, September 26 and 27. The hearings represented more of a token effort by the Subcommittee chairman, Senator Bayh, to keep the direct vote issue alive and was largely a one-man undertaking with the Senator presiding and discussing it alone with those appearing to testify. The record of 227 pages does not show that any of the minority members attended any of the sessions or that any of the minority staff was present. About four hours of time was alloted to the hearings on those two days.[17]

Present as witnesses were some of the same cast as for prior hearings. Nine individuals testified, including Senator Robert Dole, Republican of Kansas, the chairman of the Democratic Party, Robert Strauss, a representative of the League of Women Voters, the

American Bar Association, the Office of the U.S. Attorney General, and new entrants, one from the United Auto Workers, and the Brookings Institution. Repeating a visit was Professor Paul Freund of Harvard University. All witnesses favored the direct vote plan. Thus, perhaps after nearly three years, the score was even.

On December 21, the subcommittee met in executive session, a usual practice, and voted unanimously to report a direct vote resolution to the full committee. But no further action was taken during that session of the Congress.

Proponents of the direct vote plan apparently believed that it was fruitless to continue formal consideration until subsequent to the 1976 election and then perhaps only if the vote was close. There was some belief that the vote would be very close in that election in both the total national popular vote and in the electoral college. These estimates were nearly correct and gave impetus to the resumption of hearings soon after the 95th Congress convened in 1977.

As a result of some reorganization of the committee system in the Senate final selection of members of the Committee on the Judiciary and the subcommittees of that Committee was delayed. It was determined, however, that hearings on changing the method of electing the president should get underway notwithstanding and they began on January 27, 1977 in the name of the full Committee with Senator Bayh presiding. Senator Ervin was no longer in the Senate and apparently Senator Eastland, the chairman, chose to share the activity of presiding since Bayh would have presumably chaired the subcommittee had it been formed at the time. Senator Eastland presided on one of the five days of the hearings. Some of the members were only temporarily assigned to the Committee in the early part of the session.

Post-election analysis of the 1976 election showed that with a shift of less than 12,000 popular votes in Ohio and Hawaii, President Ford would have attained the needed electoral majority even though he would not have had the highest national total popular vote. With a shift of less than 15,000 popular votes in Ohio and Delaware, neither Ford nor Carter would have gained the electoral college majority making the decision a task for the House. Those projections undoubtedly dominated the reasons for the haste in the scheduling of the

hearings. They were also prompted by some reactions to
the debate over a vote by a "faithless elector" from
the state of Washington who cast his vote for Ronald
Reagan instead of Ford who had won the popular vote in
that state. This was the third consecutive election in
which there was a defecting elector.

A review of the record of the hearings in 1969,
1970, and 1973 shows that the issues were fully debated and arguments advanced pro and con clearly drawn.
The position of Committee members was generally obvious. Furthermore, the Senate had formally considered
the proposal in 1970 even though a vote was not taken.
(The record does not show Senate attendance during
those debates.)

During the period and subsequently however, changes
in the Committee membership meant that the more recently designated for service on the Committee had not
heard the testimony and if hearings were to serve a
noble purpose, then additional hearings were nearly
mandatory.

Thus, after holding hearings over much of the
prior decade and even earlier, nine additional days of
hearings were taken in 1977, but in two segments.[18]
The first was in January and February and the second in
July and August. By the latter time the subcommittees
were organized and the hearings were under the auspices
of the subcommittee concerned, now renamed the Subcommittee on the Constitution, with Senator Bayh continuing in the role of chairman.

The element of surprise occasioned by the early
start of the hearings may have been to the initial disadvantage of opponents of direct election perhaps except that witnesses from organizations or individuals
in the Washington area might have been readily available. Organizations favoring direct election had been
plentiful in prior years, but opponents had been less
successful in matching numbers. In any event, opponents
had few witnesses during the first stage of the hearings.

The January and February hearings consume nearly
450 printed pages of testimony and an additional 150
pages of exhibits and statements. Although the time
span during the five days was approximately fifteen
hours, the sessions were interrupted with recesses of
varying periods.

The witnesses invited to appear and those volunteering totaled thirty-eight with approximately one-third of them members of the House or Senate. Of the remainder, the proponents of direct election should have felt vindicated and even optimistic since of the organizations represented, only one opposed it, the U.S. Labor Party. Of the other individuals, only two objected to it.

After the February hearings period the Committee decided, and without dissent, to bring the proposal to the Senate on or before September 16, 1977. As a part of that agreement, however, additional hearings were to be held to provide opponents the opportunity to make their position known to the subcommittee. This arrangement was to establish credibility with opponents and at least inform Senators who had not already announced a position. It was intended also to insulate opponents against objecting on procedural grounds that there had not been an adequate opportunity to be heard.

The witness selection process was summarized in this way by Senator Bayh.[19] "Senator Scott [William L. Scott, Republican of Virginia, and a member of the subcommittee] has agreed to work with all of the members of the Judiciary Committee who oppose Senate Joint Resolution 1 and agree with them on the witnesses who should appear at these hearings to testify in opposition to the amendment. In addition, there will be witnesses appearing to testify in support of the amendment." The agreement further stipulated that as much as eight additional hours should be given to the taking of testimony and that there would be a balance between those favoring and those opposing the Resolution.

The second phase of the hearings commenced before the subcommittee on July 20 and concluded on August 2. The printed report consists of 288 pages and an appendix of almost 250 pages. These were nineteen witnesses, of whom two were Senators, both appearing in support of direct election. They were Senators Dole and Vermont Democrat Patrick L. Leahy. From the academic community three of four opposed. Organizations represented included the National Farmers Union supporting, and as on prior occasions, the American Farm Bureau opposing. The National Council of Jewish Women favored it, but some advertising and elections research groups indicated general opposition.

The testimony would have been quite familiar and repetitive to members of the subcommittee with prior service, but the composition of both the Committee and subcommittee had changed. Of the sixteen members of the full Committee in 1973 only seven remained. (There were seventeen members in 1977). New members of the subcommittee were Senators James Abourezk, Democrat of South Dakota, James B. Allen, Democrat of Alabama, Howard M. Metzenbaum, Democrat of Ohio, William L. Scott, Republican of Virginia, and Orrin G. Hatch, Republican of Utah.

As a result of the reorganization of the subcommittees of the Committee on the Judiciary, the Subcommittee on the Constitution in 1977 was reduced in size from eleven to six. The reduction in size was made simple, politically, at least, since the only holdover member was Senator Bayh. Of the new members on the subcommittee, Senators Abourezk and Metzenbaum are not recorded as having attended any of the hearings, although Senator Metzenbaum submitted a statement supporting direct election.

On September 15, 1977, the full committee approved the resolution by a vote of nine to eight.[20] Of the six members of the subcommittee, only three supported it, Senators Abourezk, Bayh, and Metzenbaum.

Consistent during the years of testimony was reference to the alignment of large and small states for or against direct election and claims and counterclaims of relative advantage or disadvantage to them. The vote in the full committee is of interest in that respect since those favoring it came from Indiana, Massachusetts, West Virginia, South Dakota, Delaware, Iowa, Ohio, Arizona, and Maryland. Opposition members came from the states of Mississippi, Arkansas, Alabama, South Carolina, Pennsylvania, Nevada, Utah, and Wyoming. The partisan political division shows that seven Democrats and one Republican supported it, and opposed were three Democrats and five Republicans. As did his predecessor, President Carter announced his support for the measure even though a president has no formal part in the amending process.

Notwithstanding these efforts by advocates of direct election, no further action was taken that year and none formally indicated during 1978.

Supporters of direct election apparently decided, however, that 1979 was the year to obtain a vote in the

Senate, and there were estimates that it could be favorable. Informal discussions among members of the Committee on the Judiciary and staff members caused Senator Bayh and other supporters to conclude that an attempt should be made to place the resolution for direct election on the Senate calendar without further hearings. On its face this was a logical and reasonable decision. The testimony was recent and voluminous. Surely there was enough information available to assist in making a decision.

Proponents were successful in setting the resolution for consideration on the Senate calendar and discussion about this procedure began on March 14, 1979. But strong objection was raised since the session which convened that year was a "new" Congress--although many Senators do not recognize that the Senate is "new" due in part to the substantial number, up to two-thirds, who are holdovers compared to the fresh two-year term for House members. Further objection was given that it would establish a bad precedent in by-passing an established subcommittee and committee. Added to those arguments was the fact that there were six new members of the full committee. Senator Hatch, member of the Committee on the Judiciary made this observation to the Senate. "It is wrong not to have committee hearings on this matter. To bypass the committee is, I think, to denigrate the committee process, especially when an amendment to the Constitution of the United States of America, the most important document in the history of this Nation, is involved."[21]

Supporters of the arrangement for direct Senate consideration made the plea that there had been more than a decade of hearings and it was wholly unnecessary to hold more of them. Nonetheless, on the following day an agreement was reached to hold more hearings and they commended on March 27 and concluded on April 19. The testimony of the four-day period covers 363 printed pages with an appendix of more than 200 additional pages. Although the time span is recorded to be in excess of twelve hours, the interruptions and recesses common to the hearing process meant far less time was actually devoted to the presentations and discussion.

Twenty-two individuals appeared before the subcommittee. Seven were members of the Congress. The remainder included a variety of representatives from organizations and others. Repeating earlier positions were the National Farmers Union, the American Farm

Bureau, the American Jewish Congress, the League of Women Voters, and the American Bar Association. Members of the academic community generally opposed the direct election proposal. The chairman of the Black Leadership Forum opposed it. Sometime Pennsylvania presidential elector James A. Michener supported it, while columnist George Will advocated continuing the electoral college system. The last witness was also a repeater, Theodore H. White, who re-stated his opposition against direct election.

Whether the testimony was balanced for and against or not, the fundamental issues were again made clear. (As in 1977, Senator Metzenbaum is not recorded as having attended any of the hearings. Senator Abourezk was no longer in the Senate). New members, Senators Alan K. Simpson, Republican of Wyoming, and Howard Heflin, Democrat of Alabama, did attend.

The March 15, 1979 agreement reflected two procedural features of significance for the expected summer or fall debate and Senate vote. A commitment was made by opponents that they would not filibuster as was done in 1970. Furthermore, following the hearings the resolution was to be reported back to the Senate by April 10, with majority and minority views filed by May 1. June 1 was the earliest date for possible Senate consideration.[22]

These details were endorsed by the Senate leadership and were intended to avoid a possible further clash about the handling of the hearings, possibly important for the future, and appeared to reflect a desire with or without enthusiasm by both opponents and proponents to vote the matter up or down. Both sides seemed optimistic about the outcome! On balance, the proponents had gained the most. All that was required of them was to support the request for additional hearings and give opponents an opportunity to present their views and to accept a few months delay in the proceedings. On the other hand, opponents had the most to lose if their expectations of defeat of the proposal proved to be wrong. Also, they had agreed to have a vote.

The agreement was recognized, but not quite. Debate began on June 21.[23] It was interrupted by the July 4 holiday recess. And apparently not included in the agreement was the prospect of delay with non-germane amendments. The counter-challenge was the prospect of cloture if the delay assumed the character

98

of a filibuster. However unsavory that procedure is to many Senators, it might have had a chance of success because of the March agreement to proceed to a vote. The prospect of a filibuster and cloture efforts soon ended, however, perhaps because opponents of direct election then believed that the measure would not pass.

Debate resumed on July 9 and a vote was taken the following day. Ninety-nine Senators cast their vote. The vote was fifty-one to forty-eight, far short of the required two-thirds needed for a Constitutional Amendment.[24]

No new arguments were advanced in the Senate debate. Issues now so familiar to most of them were much the same: factionalism, regionalism, splinter political parties, large and small state influences, the federal system, voting equality, fraud, runoff problems, the nominating process, nationalization of voting administration, minority advantages, the contingency arrangement, the prospect of a plurality but not a majority presidency, voter turnout, registration of voters, and the future of the two-party system and organization.

The negative votes on the resolution were cast by twenty-eight Republicans, nineteen Democrats and one Independent, and represented Senators from thirty-five states. Nine of the forty northern Democrats opposed it, and ten of the nineteen southern Democrats voted against it. The Senate chamber was often nearly empty during the debate and there appeared difficulty on occasion to have enough Senators present to use the time alloted.

Apparently most of the persuasive lobbying against the measure came from such groups as the New York based American Jewish Congress, and the Urban League. They insisted that the voting strength or advantage they had under the electoral college system would be diminished for Black and Jewish voters if the direct election plan were substituted. Other votes against the resolution were the result of concerns about a possible adverse impact on the two-party system which would fractionalize it, the heightened impact of the media, especially television, on a presidential campaign. Other negative votes reflected individual views of Senators rather than any strong constituency position. There was no evidence at the time of much national interest in the measure being debated and voted upon. Public concerns then were far greater about foreign affairs and the economy. Anyway, the next president would not be elected for more than fifteen months.

The direct election proposal had support from Senators from states widely scattered throughout the Nation. Thirty-nine Democrats and twelve Republicans voted for it. Regionally, the most concentrated support came from the midwestern Senators.[24]

Proponents had amassed support from quite diverse groups and individuals who on other issues would have opposed each other. As noted earlier, illustrative was the support of the American Civil Liberties Union and the U.S. Chamber of Commerce.

The vote was split between Senators from several states. These were Alabama, Alaska, Arizona, Arkansas, California, Connecticut, Idaho, Illinois, Indiana, Iowa, Kansas, Louisiana, Maryland, Minnesota, Missouri, Montana, New Jersey, New York, North Dakota, South Dakota, Texas, and Utah.

States with eight or more electoral votes were nearly divided, with twenty-seven opposed and twenty-six in favor.

Opponents found few so-called liberal supporters among organizations, but there were several in the Senate. Democratic Senators usually supporting such proposals but who voted against direct election included Bill Bradley of New Jersey, Daniel Patrick Moynihan of New York, Joseph R. Biden, Jr. of Delaware, John A. Dirkin of New Hampshire, Edmund S. Muskie of Maine, and Paul S. Sarbanes of Maryland. Usually liberal Republicans who voted in the negative included Charles H. Percy of Illinois, Lowell P. Weicker, Jr. of Connecticut, and John Heinz of Pennsylvania.

This Senate action should not be interpreted as a sign that there will not be a renewed effort to change the electoral college system. To the contrary. It is a matter very much alive. Its importance as a current and urgent matter may be questioned, but it is one still to be reckoned with. Only the timing for it remains uncertain and probably unpredictable.

The next chapter is designed to narrow the issues about changing the presidential selection arrangement and thereby sharpen their focus.

FOOTNOTES

1. U.S. Congress, House of Representatives, Judiciary Committee, Hearings on Electoral College Reform, 91st Cong., 1st sess., February 5, 6, 19, 20, 26, 27, March 5, 6, 12, and 13, 1969, p. 1.

2. Wise, Sidney, and Richard F. Schier, (eds.), Studies on Congress (New York: Thomas Y. Crowell Company, 1969), p. 19.

3. Morrow, William L., Congressional Committees, (New York: Charles Scribner's Sons, 1969), p. 95.

4. Truman, David, The Governmental Process, (New York: Alfred A. Knopf, 1951), p. 372.

5. Baker, John W., (ed.), Member of the House-- Letters of a Congressman by Clem Miller, (New York: Charles Scribner's Sons, 1962), p. 8.

6. Huitt, Ralph K., writing in Truman, David, (ed.), The Congress and America's Future, (Englewood Cliffs, N.J.: Prentice-Hall, 1973), p. 108.

7. Morrow, op. cit., p. 93.

8. U.S. Congress, House of Representatives, Report on Direct Popular Election of the President, 91st Cong., 1st sess., House Report 91-253, May 16, 1969.

9. Congressional Quarterly Weekly Report, (hereafter cited as CQ), September 26, 1969.

10. CQ, October 3, 1969, p. 1880.

11. 1969 Hearings, op. cit.

12. U.S. Congress, Senate, Judiciary Committee, Hearings on Electoral College Reform, 91st Cong., 2nd sess., April 15, 16, and 17, 1970, p. 7.

13. Ibid., p. 8.

14. CQ, May 1, 1970, p. 1174.

15. CQ, August 21, 1970, p. 2093.

16. _CQ_, October 9, 1970, p. 2464.

17. U.S. Congress, Senate, Judiciary Committee, Sub-committee on Constitutional Amendments, _Hearings_ on Electoral Reform, 93rd Cong., 1st sess., September 26 and 27, 1973.

18. U.S. Congress, Senate, Judiciary Committee, _Hearings_ on Electoral College and Direct Election, 95th Cong., 1st sess., January 27, February 1, 2, 7 and 10, 1977, and _Hearings_ before the Subcommittee on the Constitution, July 20, 22, 28, and August 2, 1977.

19. _Ibid._, p. 1.

20. U.S. Congress, Senate, Judiciary Committee, _Report_ on Direct Popular Election of the President and Vice President of the United States, Report no. 95-609, December 6, 1977, p. 23.

21. _Congressional Record_, vol. 125, no. 31, March 14, 1979, p. S 2713.

22. U.S. Congress, Senate, Judiciary Committee, _Report_ on Direct Popular Election of the President and Vice President of the United States, Report no. 96-111, May 1, 1979. This Report summarizes the recent history of efforts to change the method of electing the president and vice president.

23. _Congressional Record_, June 21, 1979, p. S 8201.

24. _Congressional Record_, vol. 125, no. 90, p. S 9109.

Chapter VIII. The Issues Narrowed

The 1979 _Report_ of the Senate Committee on the
Judiciary to accompany S. J. 28 on direct election of
the president includes both the majority position
favoring it and minority views opposing it. These
positions bring into focus the essentials about the
alleged defects of the electoral college, the corrective measures provided for in the Resolution, and the
claimed advantages and improvements in the presidential
selection process which would result from its adoption
and subsequent operation. (The language of the
Resolution is included in the Appendix of this volume).

Through the _Report_ members of the Committee narrow
the basic issues. Each position, majority and minority, is supported with data and reasoning. The extent
to which the case for either is made largely depends
upon the strength of the argument and the probable
views of the reader.

The majority view centers primarily upon the
shortcomings of the electoral college. These are
reduced to four: the faithless elector; the winner-
take-all system in allocating electoral votes in each
state; the contingency election arrangement in the
House; and the uncertainty that the individual with the
highest national popular vote would win the presidency.

The majority position, however, extends beyond
these considerations. On a positive theme it is
maintained that direct election would result in reasonable popular majorities, require a broad geographic
distribution of votes, strengthen the two-party system,
better serve minorities, discourage voter and vote-
counting fraud, and insure a democratic contingency
plan. And in response to some of the more pronounced
claims of opponents, the majority insists that the
plan would not weaken the federal system, be adverse
to small states, nor present new problems in the
counting of votes.

It is on these points that the majority generally
rests its case. There is brief mention of alternative
proposals including the proportional, district, automatic, and national bonus plans. These are considered
by the majority to be inadequate to the reform goals
desired or have other defects which would make them
unacceptable or less desirable.

The opponents of direct election clothe their position around the belief that there is nothing fundamentally wrong with the present system, that it is not seriously flawed in any event. To them, the defects are minor and could be altered without such drastic surgery as would be mandated under the direct election proposal. Much of the opposition, however, centers around this statement: "Direct election would create more problems than it would solve."[1]

Opponents, and many defenders of the electoral college system, recognize that the claim the electoral college does permit the election of a "runnerup" president, one who has received fewer national popular votes than one of his opponents. After all, it has happened. But at the same time they insist that this happened only once in the last 100 years, in 1888, and there was a succession in the office without internal discord and on schedule. They add that Gerald H. Ford was "elected" without having received any popular votes!

The minority portion of the Report summarizes their position which they maintained during the several years of the hearings and the 1979 Senate debate on the possible, and unknown, results of a change to the direct election plan. The spectre of these unknowns is used to strengthen their position.

They are highlighted in this way.

Seriously undermine one of the few remaining vital areas of American federalism by eliminating the role of the states in the electoral process;

Threaten the continued existence of a moderate, two party system by encouraging the poliferation of small, frequently extremist, splinter parties;

Polarize public opinion and endanger electoral minorities through a restructuring of the nature of political compromise;

Erode the popular "legitimacy" of Presidents, who, under a system of direct election, may have significant support in but a single region of the country;

Create new incentives for electoral fraud and corruption;

Sharply reduce the orderliness of the presidential transition period through interminable electoral recounts and runoff elections;

Involve the federal government far more deeply into areas of voter eligibility and election administration, currently within the purview of the states; and

Sharply increase the influence of the national media, and professional "image-makers" in Presidential elections.

For the minority, additional factors remained unanswered. These were put in the form of questions.

What will be its impact upon the Presidential nominating process?

How will it affect relationships between elected federal officials and their state party organizations?

Will state party organizations retain their same character?

What sort of role will the media play in the new presidential election system?

What sorts of coalitions will be developed among voters?

How will the relationship between the executive and legislative branches be affected?

Much of the argument about direct election during the hearings and in the debates in 1970 and 1979 in the Senate often centered upon the unpredictability of the consequences of the plan. Opponents insisted that all of the above questions, perhaps even others, had not been satisfactorily answered. As one witness put it, "The sudden abandonment of institutions is an act that reverberates in ways no one can predict and may come to regret." And a companion view was that "it must be shown beyond all reasonable doubt that the adverse consequences which are predicted by many will not occur."[2]

Proponents generally responded to these views that all consequences and all adverse effects cannot be prevented, and whatever they are or may be, the advantages of the direct vote plan far outweigh them and could not be worse than the "Rube Goldberg mechanism" or "Russian roulette" of the electoral college system.

Some uncertainties about the direct election plan are recognized by supporters. They recognize the first two of their four central positions as contained in the majority Report of 1979 are not very formidable. These are, as indicated above, the faithless elector and the general-ticket system in allocating and casting the electoral vote in each state. The former could be eliminated easily through the adoption of an automatic plan and there is good evidence that such an amendment would be ratified by the states. The latter could be changed by state action such as was done in Maine in adopting the district plan if that route would be favored. Of course, to make it uniform and insure its permanence a Constitutional amendment would be essential.

The other two planks in the majority presentation are less easily disposed of. The purists insist that the mood of Americans is not to accept henceforth a president who did not receive the highest national popular vote. This is often coupled with objections to the House contingency plan. The egalitarians are almost adamant that the House feature now existing is so wholly undemocratic that it should be summarily discarded.

Assuming corrective measures are needed, what plan or plans can be agreed to? Direct election advocates seem not to be willing to approach the issues with incremental or piecemeal solutions. It would seem that the momentum for support for direct election during the 1960s tended to drown out alternative proposals, some of which had been around for a long time.

It should be assumed, further, that some changes are highly desirable, and that the first two elements of the majority argument are needed at an early date, is piecemeal amending not preferable to nothing at all?

It has been the "faithless elector" in the 1968, 1972 and 1976 elections which produced many distress signals. Are proponents fearful that by eliminating the defectors in the electoral college the impact would be to smother the rest of the direct election argument?

Another weakness in the majority position and

often recognized by many of them is that the direct vote plan has a virtual built-in prediction that there will be runoff elections. The 40 percent feature is an obvious admission. Also discounted is that even if that requirement were always or nearly always met the Nation could still have a minority president and even most of the time.

Concerns about the adverse impact on the federal system are usually dismissed as being of little consequence or even archaic. Proponents categorically state that any claim that there is a "federal" president is ill-founded, untrue and never was true. To them the president is the only principal national officer and should be under the ultimate control of the popular will. Opponents continue to insist that the electoral college system is a sturdy bulwark of the federal design and is vital to the internal security of the Nation. It is obvious, however, that the federal system has been undergoing substantial change in recent decades primarily through the expanded use of the delegated and implied powers of the Congress with a generous assist on occasion from the U. S. Supreme Court.

Proponents give some consolation to their opposition on this latter point. Without departing from their stance on the national will they show that all is not bad, for the federal design remains otherwise generally intact. To them, there is a balance in the House and the Senate with House districts arranged by the states and members so elected protect and promote local interests in each state. The Senate also provides for members from individual states and on a state equality basis and they perform similarly for statewide interests. What is often overlooked in the discussion of the federal design is that the 10th Amendment citing reserve powers to the states is of little significance today in any attempt to check some of the possible excesses of congressional actions.

It is somewhat curious that proponents maintain that minorities would not suffer and lose a present possible advantage while at the same time opponents insist that they would. The vote in the Senate by some members on July 10, 1979 would tend to support the views of opponents of the direct vote plan.

The majority position included the argument that "reasonable majorities" would result in a national vote tally for the presidency. This was a reference to the allegation that the direct vote would produce possible tyrannical majorities and be "abusive of the rights of minorities." Opponents address the question of majorities in a different way saying that a president could be elected who gained his plurality in only one region, such as in large metropolitan areas in a few large states and would not represent a broadly based mandate. Proponents counter that there have never been sectional presidents and the change would make "national" presidents the general rule.

Of the opponents' unanswered questions and one considered repeatedly through the hearings in the Senate committee or subcommittee concerned the two-party system. Advocates of direct election maintained that the electoral college system has little bearing on the long history of the two-party dominance and does not result from it. Opponents counter that third parties have existed throughout most of the history of presidential elections and some with much strength even though winning the presidency was rarely their goal. If the direct election proposal was not fostering third party strength and at the expense of the two-party system, then why the 40 percent rule?

Much rhetoric flowed about the impact of direct election on the small states in the hearings. Senator Bayh particularly endeavored to dismiss the claim of relative advantage or disadvantage in either large or small states through the elector college system. In his opening remarks in the 1979 hearings, he made this comment. "Before we begin, I would like to give notice that there is one kind of argument made on this topic with which I must confess I have become increasingly impatient, and that is, who is advantaged and who is disadvantaged under the electoral college."[3] His impatience did not foreclose further discussion. Opponents responded that there is a substantial difference between a simple arithmetic advantage of electoral votes and "useful political power." Small states may have some extra influence through the electoral vote system which could be impaired or "lost" under a national popular vote system. In the 1979 Senate vote on the direct vote amendment the division was not small-state versus large-state Senators. Indeed, twenty-two sponsors of the Resolution were from states with nine or fewer electoral votes.

Although apparently not high on the list of priorities given in the Report, fraud in elections was discussed frequently during the hearings and debates.

Both proponents and opponents of direct vote seemed to agree that early attention should be given to the subject. The age-old criticism that a shift in a few votes here and there would change the election under the electoral college system, if by fraud in the voting or the counting, was indeed valid and should be eliminated if at all possible. The entire question of a wrong recount, for whatever reason, was put into clear focus by Professor L. Kinvin Wroth of the University of Maine in his testimony in 1977.[4] His analysis was that there is immediate and nearly urgent need to revamp the entire system for the handling of recounts and election contests. He left open whether there should be a highly centralized national system or whether the state and federal courts could handle it. He showed that whether a change in the system of election of the president came about or not the need was still there. At best, the statutes covering recounts and contests, nation-wide, are most inadequate.

The House contingency method has long been the object of disaffection by many. The very idea of one vote for each state is virtually repulsive to some. Added to that is the claimed adverse impact on the doctrine of the separation of powers and the prospect that a president so selected would have an undue dependency or obligation to the House or some of its members. The possible solutions have been given if a contingency method remained in the Congress.

One element may arise as an issue which is not usually associated with proposals to change the method of electing the president. Has the electoral college system become a Republican institution? A rather simple analysis will show, even if it is inconclusive and short range, that seventeen of nineteen western states have favored Republican candidates in recent elections. The other two are Hawaii and Texas with the latter less predictable. The state by state populations, or even in a combined total, are relatively low, except for California and Texas, but the possible electoral vote advantage provides up to about 45 percent of the electoral votes needed to win. With probable increases in population, primarily through internal migration, in the areas involved, the proportion could well increase. In earlier years the "solid south" was looked upon in a similar fashion as favoring the Democratic candidate rather consistently.

It is apparent that the challengers and the challenged are far apart in finding agreeable solutions.

Perhaps that is the very essence of a democratic political system. In fashioning presidential elections the goals are often obscured by the route to be taken. The framers knew that in 1787 when the electoral college was invented. Does it really matter, however, whether the system now works as the framers intended or whether they knew how it would work? It is the contention of defenders that it has worked and has worked continuously and under almost every possible circumstance.

The next chapter is a summary defense of the electoral college system.

FOOTNOTES

1. 1979 Report, op. cit., p. 43.

2. Ibid., p. 44.

3. Ibid., p. 2.

4. Op. cit., pp. 122-132.

Chapter IX. A Defense of the Electoral College

"If it ain't broke, don't fix it." That is a frequent chant of defenders of the electoral college system. They point out that the system has worked continuously, has produced a president each four years and he has taken office on schedule. They are not always inclined, however, to emphasize some of the difficulties which have arisen from time to time and fail to satisfy critics who insist that however good it has been, it could easily falter and therefore it is time for a change and one is long overdue.

The most severe critics have called the electoral college arrangement archaic, undemocratic, complex, ambiguous, indirect, and dangerous.[1] Others describe it as having been "neither an exercise in applied Platonism nor an experiment in indirect government based on elitist distrust of the masses. It was merely a jerry-rigged improvision which has subsequently been endowed with a high theoretical content. . . The vital aspect of the electoral college was that it got the Convention over the hurdle and protected everybody's interests."[2]

It has also been described as a hoary and outworn relic of the stagecoach era and an abortive organism. Others have called it a loaded pistol aimed at our system of government.

Justice Robert H. Jackson of the U. S. Supreme Court took occasion in 1952 to state that "as an institution the Electoral College suffered atrophy almost indistinguishable from _rigor_ _mortis_."[3]

With such stinging criticisms of the system for electing the president and which have been repeated frequently in recent years, it is surprising that even some minor piecemeal changes have not been forthcoming.

Supporters of the electoral college system generally agree that its continuation for so long is a sterling tribute to it, and that the system it provided has functioned with but minor skirmishes--a most remarkable achievement. As presented earlier, the independence of the elector has been modified over the passing of time, mainly by practice, but not made wholly perfunctory. The general-ticket system or unit rule gradually evolved as the dominate method of selecting the electors. Furthermore, the Congress, although not totally, almost always respects the votes as certified from the several states. Election machinery, including nominations and the rules about candidacy, has remained primarily in the hands of the states where it was in the beginning.

The challenges to the electoral college have already been reviewed and compared with other proposals. Real or alleged weaknesses have been presented. Nonetheless, a defense of the current presidential election system is warranted.

The essentials of the electoral college system are easily stated and have been referred to earlier. But it should be observed that the electoral college is not a "college" and the word "college" does not appear in the U. S. Constitution. Furthermore, the electors do not assemble in one place to perform their singular duty, but rather act individually in each state on the day fixed by the Congress. The choice, according to Hamilton, was to provide a "detached and divided situation [which] will expose them to much less heat and ferments, which might be communicated from them to the people, than if they were all to be convened at one time, in one place."[4] It is easy to speculate what different results might have been realized had there been a national assembly of electors from the beginning.

The simplicity of the electoral college is evidenced by the formula used to allocate electoral votes to each state, based on a two-fold method: population for the vast majority of them, and state equality. This allocation formula has remained unchanged from the beginning except for the inclusion of the District of Columbia by Constitutional amendment. Also from the beginning, the total national popular vote has been of little positive significance in determining the outcome. Rather, it is a gaining of a majority of electoral votes nation-wide which has been the challenge to candidates and political parties. And whether announced by handbill, newspaper, radio, telegraph, or television, the results on election night or soon thereafter have been through state-by-state electoral vote tabulations. Theodore H. White made this observation in the hearings in 1970 about the popular vote. He said, "It may amuse you to know in all the years since then [1960] I have never been able to get an official count of John F. Kennedy's margin over Richard Nixon. One count says 113,000, the Clerk of the House says 119,450; there is another count of 112,000, another count of 122,000. There is no way now of collecting a direct official vote in the United States of America."[5]

White may have exaggerated. Presumably there are ways to obtain a correct count, or at least to determine an official count.

(Another consistent characteristic of the electoral college system is the extension of state equality in the contingency feature in the event no electoral college majority is attained by any candidate.) If the electors fail, they are of no further use, having fulfilled their only function, that of casting their votes. It is not wholly clear why the framers of the Constitution provided for this kind of a contingency plan with each state having one vote, but it may have been associated with other compromises of the time between large and small states. If a runoff was even considered, the time span available between November and March may have been presumed to be sufficient, but transportation and communications were indeed slow in those days, nation-wide.

The Congress has given procedural direction in the use of the contingency feature and has been called upon on a few occasions to determine what to do with defectors votes: tabulate them as cast, or rule otherwise. Apparently the Congress has not bound itself to absolutely "rubber stamp" the electoral count it receives.

The states have maintained their wide latitude in determining the manner in which they select the person of elector, and during this century, except in Maine since 1972, the winning electors have been those under the unit rule or general-ticket system. Interestingly, the names of electors do not appear on all ballots and they are selected, presumably for the most part, as a political reward for party activity and loyalty. In some states a write-in for president is permitted in balloting, but may require that the names of electors also be provided. In any event, it would seem rare indeed to learn of any prospective elector who did much public campaigning for the position.

Some states, but not all, have wrestled with the problem of preventing defectors and to insure that the electors vote in accordance with the popular vote decision, a plurality or majority. These efforts, of course, have not been wholly successful. It is made somewhat difficult since the apparent original intent of the framers was to rest the decision with the electors as individuals of superior discernment and free to choose among the candidates. The intent of the framers notwithstanding, a further difficulty has resulted from the general acceptance by the Congress of the votes of defectors.

Senator Thomas Hart Benton observed in the 1820s that although the intent of the framers was to rest the decision within the elector's discretion, it had not worked out that way. He said that "this invention has failed of its objective in every election is a fact of such universal notoriety, that no one can dispute it. That it ought to have failed is equally uncontestable; for such independence in the electors was wholly incompatible with the safety of the people. . . was in fact a chimerical and impractical idea in any community."[6]

A review of elections since Benton's time may put differing emphasis on his conclusions, but the degree of failure and promotion of insecurity of the people is questionable. No insurrections have resulted.

Actions by the electors are toward the end of the selection system. The few defectors have caused but minor ripples in the system. What happens prior to the actions by the electors is at the heart of it. Basic to any election system is candidacy. With the rise of the political party, the subsequent development of the nominating conventions, and more recently the rather rapid extension of the state system of presidential primaries, the drama of election campaigning and election night results are obviously preceeded or companions to a host of other activities, some beginning years before the final event. In this century and primarily in recent decades advances in means of communication, primarily television, and transportation, primarily air travel, have accelerated these developments. Their impact on the entire political process in presidential selection has intensified competition for the office of president on a national and state and regional scale which would have been quite beyond the imagination of the most perceptive of the founding fathers.

Defenders of the electoral college system insist that it is a simple arrangement. The number of votes

in the electoral college is fixed in advance. Each
voter can know, therefore, how many electoral votes he
helps in deciding. The state by state allocation is
altered, if at all, only after each decennial census
and these changes usually affect but a very small
proportion of the total House seats and also thereby
changing the number of electoral votes. The number of
states affected, however, has ranged from eleven to
half of them since 1940.

One of the most skilled treatments of the electoral college system was by the late Martin Diamond in
1977. In response to the allegation that it is an
archaic system he said that "it is the very model of
up-to-date constitutional flexibility." His summary is
succinct.[7]

> Perhaps no other feature of the Constitution
> has had a greater capacity for dynamic historical
> adaptiveness. The electors became nullities;
> presidential elections became dramatic national
> contests; the federal elements in the process
> became strengthened by the general-ticket practice
> (that is, winner-take-all); modern mass political
> parties developed; campaigning moved from rather
> rigid sectionalism to the complexities of a
> modern technological society--and all this
> occurred tranquilly and legitimately within the
> original constitutional framework (as modified by
> the Twelfth Amendment).

One of the great strengths of the U. S. Constitution and the government it provides is for both
continuity and change. The arrangements for government
were and continue to be the result of compromises among
the forces which shape them. The plan was to prevent
a wholly centralized or national governmental system
in the belief that if that were the course it would
prove to be dangerously responsive to temporary but
strong national moods and damage both the stability
and continuity of government, even society itself.
The compromises agreed to by the framers are obvious
and well known. Much of the pattern for government
resulted from responses to issues between large and
small states and between those who wanted to continue
some sort of loose federation and those seeking a
stronger centralized national republic. One major
result was provision to prevent too much political
power from being positioned in one single element of
government. The arrangements for the Congress are
illustrative whereby the principle of state equality

was insured. The executive power was made singular and vested in a president. To further the federal design, the electoral college was "invented" and made a logical sequence of the place of the states in the Union. And to further hedge against the concentration of power in one branch of government the mix can be character- ized as a system of shared and divided powers not only within the central government, but also for the component states which were already in place.

This governmental mix and the powers granted, or available, or denied, are at the heart of the U. S. federal system. That the system imposed some con- straints on what might be otherwise rapid movements by the governmental enterprise and result in some excesses have long disturbed many in our midst who believe that the system is antiquated and in need of drastic over- haul to make it more responsive to the needs of the people, or some of them. That criticism is carried by these critics into the method by which we elect the president since it is the federal design which is at its center. Diamond put it this way: "It makes the states dramatically and persuasively important in the whole presidential selection process, from the earliest strategies in the nominating campaign through the convention and final election."[8]

It is not surprising therefore that supporters of the electoral college believe that continuing the federal system is far more vital to the future security of the United States than unbridled egalitarianism. Few among them would view with distress that the system is old style and in need of an entirely new model. Neither would most of them believe that there was and should be some neat division of powers between the states and the central government which was or should be etched in granite. Nor would they likely argue very strongly for some of the vestiges of dual federal- ism save for a few who support states rights in the extreme. The very fabric of the entire system remains, often stubbornly, <u>federal</u> even though it no longer resembles the original character.

(Defenders of the electoral college believe they are only supporting a very basic ingredient of demo- cratic government and <u>representative</u> government and that the electoral college sends what has been called a federalizing impulse throughout our whole political process.)

Is the system now prevailing so undemocratic that

it is totally incompatible with the possible fulfillment of society's goals? Diamond insists that presidential elections are already democratic.

> We already have one-man, one vote--but in the states. Elections are as freely and democratically contested as elections can be--but in the states. Victory always goes democratically to the winner of the raw popular vote--but in the states. The label given to the proposed reform, "direct popular election," is a misnomer; the elections have already become as directly popular as they can be--but in the states.[9]

This conclusion is reached: that to abolish the participation of the states in the process is not to make elections more democratic, but rather to make them more directly national. The question can be put: are the people of the United States actually displeased with an election arrangement which is partly federal, not wholly national? Is a national referendum the wanted route to insure a people's choice? To this time there is no national referendum, per se, for any purpose.

Generally, the U. S. House of Representatives has been regarded as a democratically selected group and made more so in recent times primarily because of a surge of judicial pronouncements on reapportionment. Some purists note that the more sparsely populated states have at least one member regardless of its size and this gives them an advantage. But the spirit does not seem willing to view the Senate in a similar fashion wherein the argument is even more applicable. But the matter is not easily ignored. If the election of the president is shifted away from the states through a nationalizing process, then why not proceed to democratize the Senate likewise? Indeed, why not ignore the states completely and establish regional districts for both houses and without particular reference to the geographic boundaries of the states?

Opponents of the electoral college counter quickly that these are quite different subjects and the election of members of the Congress represents a representative system and a great number of individuals to be elected, whereas the election of the chief executive is about the selection of but one individual who is solely national and should be from one vast national constituency. Not so, say defenders of the electoral college system. Rather the office of president is federal, in part, and national, in part.

Separate issues or not, there remain some separate
considerations not to be easily ignored. Is ours a
pluralistic society? If so, then the federal system
is necessary to insure its continuation. That system
makes possible one which is responsive to diverse
interests, reflecting diverse opinions, and thereby
produce varied and even conflicting results. But it
provides not some national uniform prescription, but a
blend resulting from ultimate consensus among us to a
high degree. It recognizes that there are sectional or
regional differences and needs which could be submerged
under a nationalizing process.

(Although no other system for electing the president has ever been used, and millions of voters
participate in it each four years, opponents allege
that it is too complex and not very well understood.)
Has its long use bred too much familiarity and therefore contempt for it? Assume, however, that it may not
be universally known to all voters and that millions
in the population do believe that the total national
popular vote determines who will be president. Is
simplicity in all things governmental and political to
be the rule? Is the "executive power" a simply
understood concept? Ask for a substantive explanation
of "judicial review" and its application and the
results of that development. Are the answers laden
with simplicity? Are the "separation of powers" and
"shared powers" elementary phrases? Who among us
fully understands the Bill of Rights and fundamental
issues arising from their application? Are they to
be scrapped because they are not simple and lacking
in that which is commonplace knowledge?

Further, voice the critics, even if it has been in
long use and may not be as complex as other features
of the governmental enterprise, then it is at least
inconvenient to use. Its inconvenience would seem to
be reflected mostly in the excesses of rhetoric along
the way.

(Supporters of the electoral college system express
deep concern about the uncertainties which could or
might arise if it were abolished.) They are disturbed
about those uncertainties and the impact they might
have on the entire political structure. They outline
the certainties of the present system and at the same
time raise a number of questions about a different
system. Assuming, for example, that the 40 percent

rule would be used and the voting results were that and little more. Would this mean a "clear mandate" to govern? In "squeaker" close elections and narrow percentage divisions between the two top contenders would there be a clear victory? Would there be uncertainties in very close elections that the plurality obtained by the candidate with the highest vote was not based on some errors along the way, fraud or not? And how can a "reform" be one calculated on the election of a minority president, albeit a plurality one?

Is the charge valid that the electoral college arrangement is dangerous? A major danger in the process, however remote, is that an outgoing president might not wish to be succeeded especially by a campaign opponent. But for some personal miff between some outgoing and incoming presidents, the oath of office has proceeded peacefully and according to the Constitutional outline. Any ripples of discontent have not left much of an imprint or produced lasting distress.

Reference has been made to the claims and counterclaims about the effects of the present system and any successor system on the two-party system. Proof of positions stated is difficult if not impossible to arrive at. But the strengths or weaknesses of the two-party system under the electoral college plan are more readily discernible and are of long-standing belief. Defenders of the present system generally argue that while third parties are possible, the more vigorous the two-party system, the more likely the majority electoral winner will be from one of the two major parties. It is said that the basic strength of the two-party characteristic is that it has the tendency to stabilize political movements, consolidate different positions and diminish extremes in the political spectrum. Electoral college adherents maintain that the electoral college and the two-party dominance are geared well and to remove the former would be to the detriment of the latter.

Campaigns are in large part directed toward obtaining party follower consensus and support especially needed after a nomination is concluded. To eliminate the electoral vote system would invite, indeed might insure, the splintering of the votes in several ways and encourage ideological parties, sectional ones, and even ethnic group parties, since each candidate (and each party on the ballot) would have a positive chance at some portion of the final tally if the direct vote, for example, were substituted. Defenders of the electoral college maintain that it is wholly inconsistent to believe that the alternative proposal of the direct vote would preserve the foundation for two-party dominance. If there is to be a majority decision why put in the 40 percent rule and the runoff contingency? A majority is not contemplated.

While all but the most dissatisfied find some accommodation within one of the major parties, under a different plan for election dissidents could readily break away and third party candidates could pick up substantial support throughout the Nation. Would such bolting become habitual? Would this kind of defection promote democratic goals and assist in realizing them? Some observers express concern that a multiplicity of parties would develop and those existing would expand and such possibilities would increase the changes of militancy and unrest which could expand into the entire body politic. No one suggests the prospect of insurrection, but rather the possibilities of wide-spread realignment of groups which combine to form the major parties.

The impact of opinion poll results on voter attitudes cannot be overlooked. Whatever the number and strengths of third parties, supporters could see that their candidates would have little chance of success under the present system and would ultimately vote for one of the major candidates. Not all would, but goodly numbers. Under a different system would that tendency prevail? If a third party of consequence is now looked upon mainly as a spoiler, would desertions from one occur under the direct vote plan? Why desert if enough votes were cast to prevent the required 40 percent from being realized? A runoff would be favorable to third party groups since the two contenders in it would find it necessary to appeal to supporters and candidates of at least some of the losers.

Close elections have occurred and have been cited. The present electoral arrangement is not structured to prevent them. Reports abound which have reconstructed some of these close elections to show that this or that might have happened if some voters had not voted as they did. This is not to dispute that kind of exercise. For example, if about 3,800 votes had been cast for Charles Evans Hughes in California in 1916 instead of for the electors for Woodrow Wilson, then Hughes would have received a majority of the electoral votes. Often cited also is the election of 1960 when if some 100,000 votes had been cast for Nixon in some five states he would have been elected instead of Kennedy. And eighty years earlier, if some 10,000 votes had been marked in New York for Winfield S. Hancock he would have won that state and thereby been the president instead of James A. Garfield.

Similar calculations have been made for other elections and serve only to show that the elections were indeed somewhat close. Critics frequently state that in such close elections the actual decision could have been made because of some irregularities here and there in one or more states. Would some other system such as the direct vote provide greater assurance that irregularities would be ended or so minimized that any which occurred would have little or no effect on the outcome? Theodore H. White testified in the 1979 Senate hearings that he found any national pool "scary." He observed:[10] "I think Illinois and Texas probably have staged some of the most crooked elections in American history. . ." If true, in a close election tally, the "crooks" would have decided the election. White pursued the matter further: ". . . if a vote is stolen in Cook County, Ill., it doesn't affect my vote in Bridgeport, Conn. That is a thing for the people of Illinois to worry about. But if the boys there in Cook County are going to start stealing votes on me, back there in Connecticut, I could be tempted to support a little vote stealing. . . You will have Federal counting of the election. . ." in a direct vote plan. However valid are the commentaries about voting irregularities wherever and whenever they occur, methods should be employed to prevent them regardless of the election plan.

A related but less significant issue about the electoral college method is the speed in determining the result. Undoubtedly the pressure on election officials is substantial and many counting errors result from the work of weary personnel, however unintentional. Even the use of technology for voting and counting does not insure there will not be errors. Recounts or tabulation reruns may not be avoidable and delays will result in determining the outcome. The 1960 election illustrated the hazard of speed in making and announcing the voting results. Hawaii was certified after that election as having cast its popular vote for the Nixon electors. This decision was contested in the courts and a judicially ordered recount for all precincts in the state reversed the original result and placed the vote in Kennedy's column. But the recount did not occur until after the electors had met as required. The Congress, the following January, was faced with two certifications, albeit the first tainted because of the judicially determined recount. The Congress decided to accept the results of the recount and the vote was certified for Kennedy. In that same election Kennedy had won the Illinois electoral vote by a narrow popular vote margin of some 9,000 votes out of a total of about 4,500,000. But there were allegations of fraud in Cook County. A Republican challenge was not pursued presumably because a recount could not have been completed until after the scheduled date for the new president to take office the following January.

This recitation of election counting problems should be a separate issue under any system. Ultimately it is the Congress which decides the election in accepting certifications of the electoral college votes from the states. Defenders of the electoral college agree with Judith Best who put it this way: "There is something to be said for a system that sharply limits the number of votes likely to be contested, that compartmentalizes and separates the votes of honest and dishonest states."[11] To her, the present system does that and there is no assurance that the direct vote plan would improve upon it.

Although it can be expected that the theories of relative advantage and disadvantage under the electoral college system will remain unabated, they continue to provide at least a limited medium for airing political differences and campaigning which might be subverted under a different system. Would a different system reduce or greatly modify the kind of recent appeals made to voters because of the elimination of the claimed current disparities cited? If so, then in what fashion? It is doubtful that many voters even consider that their state has any particular advantage or disadvantage in the current system. Anyway, as Best observes, the presidency is but one power center in the governmental system.

Best concludes her defense of the electoral college with criteria for a desired presidential election system.[12]

First, an electoral system should produce a definite, accepted winner and avoid prolonged contests and disputes that create uncertainty and public turmoil;

Second, an electoral system should preserve the prestige, power, and potential for leadership of the office of the President;

Third, an electoral system should support our nonideological two-party system;

Fourth, an electoral system should preserve federalism.

Finally, an electoral system should provide effective representation and political equality. (The present system does not provide arithmetic equality; it does not provide each voter with an equally weighted vote. Political equality, however, involves much more than the strictly logical application of an oversimplified principle).

Critics of the electoral college would not accept these criteria as being adequate to describe the most desirable method of electing the president. Indeed, they would cite them as not only falling far short but actually highlighting the shortcomings of the present system. Nor could they react positively to the New York Times editorial about the electoral college published the day prior to the Senate vote in 1979 on the direct vote proposal.[13]

To elect a President, even arrogant majorities must be solicitous of minorities; even alienated minorities must work with majorities. The system encourages moderation in radical times and protects against parochial passions. It discourages minor parties yet rewards their protest with majority-party attentiveness. It is widely understood and accepted. It is a bond with history, a source of stability. . .

The desirable amendment would abolish the flesh-and-blood electors and yet retain the counting of electoral votes. Why change what works?

The next chapter is a plan for electoral change.

FOOTNOTES

1. American Bar Association Report of the Commission on Electoral College Reform, Electing the President, p. 3, included in the 1977 Senate Hearings.

2. 1977 Senate Hearings, op. cit., p. 90.

3. Ray v. Blair, 343 U. S. 214, 232 (1952).

4. Federalist No. 68.

5. 1970 Senate Hearings, op. cit., p. 29.

6. Quoted in Senate Document 92-82, 92nd Cong., 2d sess., p. 443.

7. 1977 Senate Hearings, op. cit., p. 165.

8. Ibid., p. 170.

9. Ibid.

10. Op. cit., pp. 348, 353.

11. Best, Judith, The Case Against Direct Election of the President--A Defense of the Electoral College, (Ithaca, N. Y.: Cornell University Press, 1971), p. 204.

12. Ibid., pp. 210-215.

13. New York Times, July 9, 1979, p. A16.

Chapter X. A Pattern for Change

Since the advocates of the direct election proposal could not muster adequate strength as late as
the Senate vote in 1979 for possible submission of it
to the states for ratification, a more modest approach
or a series of efforts should be put in motion to
achieve some changes in the method of electing the
president.

One pattern for change is an incremental approach.
If done, the results could be tested in each succeeding
presidential election and appraisals made to determine
the wisdom and success of the action taken.

If this approach had been followed and made effective as late as the 1972 election there would by 1981
have been three results to review. The evidence from
them would be far more convincing to those supporting
varying positions about altering the selection system
than has been available otherwise. Critics of the
various alternative plans would quickly state, of
course, that the results of many prior elections have
been thoroughly reviewed. It is true that extensive
translations have been done, but these have been
primarily numerical or mechanical ones, and have generally ignored the likely prospect that campaigns and
voting, for example, would have been quite different
had some other electoral plan been in effect at the
time of each election.

All but the most enthusiastic supporters of direct
election acknowledge that the plan would provide an
entirely different set of unknown procedures and
possibly unforseen results. Even critics of direct
election know they cannot predict with accuracy many
of their apprehensions about the effects and impact
from its use. But some proponents do not devote such
effort at sounding them out at all.

It is time to find some setting away from the
atmosphere of the committee hearing room for the
leaders of the several alternative plans to join in an
approach for changing the elector system without the
single theme of either a plan for direct election or
one which about retains the status quo. In addition
to members of the Congress there should be leaders from
some state legislatures, state political party leaders,
other public officials, members of the general public,

and from the academic community. This group need not be large and possibly therefore unwieldly, but large enough to make for broad public representation and permit concensus, and from it to bring a high degree of unity for proposals and sustained effort toward ultimate ratification of them.

There should be little difficulty in proposing an amendment to abolish the human office of elector to insure that electoral votes would be cast automatically for the candidate who received the majority or plurality of the popular vote in each state. Such action, after ratification, would end the morning-after distresses and speculation whether there might be faithless electors in December (there were none in 1980) and also bring to a conclusion the spirited discourse which would follow if there were some. In this way a long chapter in the history of electing the president could be given a dignified burial. Hopefully it would also be a quiet burial since the electors have successively produced a president for a long time who would have won anyway if the automatic feature had been the rule.

With the most recent elections easily recalled, members of the Congress and the state legislatures should find it extremely difficult to object to this rather simple alteration. The most partisan proponents of direct election might object since this change would remove the quadrennial distress signals and oratory which have accompanied the post-election canvassing of electoral votes each fourth January by the Congress. One of their rallying cries would be gone.

A second challenge to the present electoral plan could be presented as a companion to the first or done subsequently. This proposal would alter the contingency feature. Now if there is no electoral majority, the Constitution requires that the decision be made by the House with each state having one vote. By statute each state delegation determines the direction of that vote. Only a few advocates of direct election believe there should be no contingency plan of some sort. Members of the Congress, especially in the House, might approve a proposal for moderate change in the present arrangement if they retained some voice in a successor plan since it has always been the responsibility of the House even though used only once. (It should be recalled, however, that in 1969 the House voted 339-70 for the direct vote plan with the runoff feature only as the contingency plan). To gain support in the

Senate a contingency plan could provide that each
member of the Congress, Senate and House, have one vote
in a joint session to make the decision. A simple
alternative, long recommended, is to leave that task
to the House but to give each member one vote.

Any reading of the hearings and the debates and
writings about electoral change shows wide differences
about a contingency feature. Direct election advocates
would end any arrangement for congressional participation. Basic to their position is that voting would be
along party lines or if not there would be much
"wheeling and dealing" between congressional leaders
and members and the presidential candidates involved.
Wallace's blunt comment did not preclude such possibilities, but he apparently wanted them to come from
the presidential electors and not from the House.

Allegations that the selection of a president by
the House or the House and Senate in some form would
make the president so selected unduly subservient to
the Congress, thereby compromising the doctrine and
practice of the separation of powers overlooks the historical record. Relations between presidents and
members of the Congress have generally taken on varying
degrees of compromise, commitment, and related arrangements in furthering presidential programs.

The contingency plan suggested here could be
presented in tandem with the automatic plan or combined
with it. To combine them, however, might mean defeat
for the whole package because of opposition to one but
not to the other. The two are not interdependent and
it would not unduly clutter the Constitution to have
two amendments instead of one additional. If both were
adopted then two of the major objections by friend and
foe of the present system would have been altered.

Neither of these proposals strikes at the heart of
the theme that even if they were adopted there is no
guarantee that the candidate with the highest popular
vote, nationally, would be elected. The direct vote
plan is claimed to correct this. Interestingly, a
contingency runoff could produce a president who was
not the highest vote getter in the initial election.
With only two candidates in a runoff the other candidate or candidates of the first election might decide
to "sit out" the runoff and give only limited support
to either candidate. Thus, a candidate with 35% of
the vote and the other with 20% might produce the
latter as the runoff winner. This does not violate the

guarantee of a majority decision, however.

A next step in the piecemeal approach could be to alter the blanket ticket or winner-take-all system in allocating the electoral vote in each state. Present Constitutional provisions permit, as they have always permitted, each state to determine what system is used. Several variations could be explored if national uniformity is deemed essential. Whether this be the goal or not, there should be a thorough examination of the Maine district plan. A district plan would recognize local interests wherein the blanket system minimizes them. The debate would continue whether emphasis on local interests by presidential candidates is desirable or to be avoided.

Another variable would be to eliminate the "constant two" electoral votes based on the Senate equality feature. This would only partially satisfy the egalitarians but it would remove one of their most frequently presented objections to the electoral college vote allocation now existing.

A district plan could mostly reflect the Maine experience or modify it with the variable. The latter would find some objection by the smaller states who would lose two votes in the process. The loss by the larger states would be less severe, of course.

Assuming the faithless elector were done away with, the contingency plan modified--but a congressional feature retained--and a district plan or something similar to the Maine plan adopted, a next step could be to examine the issue about partisanship prevailing in designating House districts as the districts also for electoral allocations. Political gerrymandering does exist in some areas. Gerrymandering adverse to ethnic groups also exists. But it is doubtful that all gerrymandering can be eliminated. Most states have continued to lodge the task of arranging districts for the election of their state legislators to the legislature itself. A few have assigned the task to a commission or similar body. Future districting for the House could be shifted to some group not involving the legislature or in some combination. If this kind of political surgery is not acceptable or unattainable, separate electoral vote districts should be provided with authority to design them granted to a state commission or left to the legislature, or perhaps in some combination. Having two districts embracing different areas in whole or in part within a state, one for the House and the other for the electoral vote, would not seem to be very essential and would unnecessarily complicate election administration.

On their face, these proposals, if done in sequence, in tandem or in combinations would appear to have primarily procedural or cosmetic effects. But if in place they would already have had a measurable impact on the presidential selection process. Some of the results would demonstrate that the changes were substantive, as well as corrective.

To supporters of the present electoral arrangement these changes would not put the federal design in distress. There could be some impact on the political party system, already under stress, but this should not be of major consequence. These proposals obviously do not embrace issues about election administration and do not address the nominating system at all.

Although the proposals presented above recommend that specific steps be taken, the sequence is not vital. The adoption of one can be independent of another. What matters ultimately is acceptance. No Constitutional amendments on the subjects at hand have emerged from the Congress during the last decade notwithstanding concentrated and continuing effort to produce one or more. It is essential that any proposal be tested for its political feasibility and ultimate success in the ratification route.

Constitutional changes cannot rest solely on the positive or negative estimates of adoption. Criteria for altering the document must accompany them. In reviewing proposals which have been advanced over the years the criteria developed by others was presented and analyzed. The proposals in this chapter vary from many of them and the following should be considered as guidelines in advancing the specific steps recommended.

1) continue the present broadly based franchise and encourage the states to correct deficiencies in statutes and in administration which tend to impair freedom to vote or not to vote;

2) minimize changes which would disrupt the long-standing and familiar electoral arrangement by preserving the federal design;

3) strengthen the political party system by insuring maximum freedom to the states in regulating that system and institute measures to strengthen political party organizations where weak or ineffective;

4) reduce the trend toward nationalization of the processes for selecting delegates to national party conventions by recognizing a stronger measure of state control, but encourage the states to reduce the opportunity for ideological advantage in those selections;

5) review the presidential primary system which may be transforming the national party conventions into mere ratifying organizations in selecting party candidates;

6) re-examine the standards for the media, especially television, as a preventive toward media domination of the nominating process and presidential campaigns;

7) encourage the states to review statutes governing the casting and counting of popular votes to eliminate the chances of fraud or other errors and cooperate as necessary with the Congress to overhaul the system for recounts and challenges, with the objective that a decision will be made of the winning candidate with a minimum of delay;

8) provide for a majority decision in the final presidential selection process.

Underlying all criteria and guidelines should be a basic goal to insure that whatever is done is in harmony with democratic ideals. That some elements of a plan do not embrace pure democracy should bring no apology.

The story can be recalled that when Benjamin Franklin emerged from the last session of the constitutional convention in 1787 he was asked by a passerby: "What kind of government have you given us, Dr. Franklin?" His reply, "A republic, Madam, if you can keep it."

Chapter XI.   Conclusions

Undoubtedly the direct vote proposal again will be the subject of national attention. Its supporters are numerous and persuasive. Whether the timing for it will precede or follow a future close election is naturally uncertain, but recent experience shows that concentrated interest follows such elections.

Advocates of direct popular vote rest their case not on the basis of very solid proof and leave suspended many unanswered questions about the proposal in operation. Indeed, this small volume has its roots in a conclusion that the unanswered questions are paramount and fundamental and cannot be readily cast aside.

Objections to an incremental approach to changing the method of electing the president have been stated. It should be noted again that underlying these objections is the position that the Constitution should not be the subject of amendment to make minor or frequent changes. One should not quarrel with that view. Recent history, however, does not support that position with what has actually happened. Since World War II several amendments have been adopted affecting the presidency. These include the 22nd for term of office limitation; the 23rd authorizing electoral votes for the District; the 24th prohibiting the non-payment of poll taxes (or other taxes) to deny the franchise to an otherwise eligible voter; the 25th concerning presidential disability; and the 26th setting a uniform minimum age for voting. None of these affected the "executive power", but they all concerned presidential selection and are not of minor consequence. These amendments clearly show that an incremental approach to Constitutional change is a practice and has not produced a chamber of horrors.

Meanwhile, the electoral college system continues to produce presidents and under a principle of majority rule.

APPENDIX

Bibliographic Note

Much of the material used in this volume is based on the House and Senate hearings beginning in 1969 and concluding in 1979. The printed Hearings total several thousand pages of testimony, statements, materials reprinted which appeared earlier elsewhere, and election data. The Hearings are available generally only in depository libraries and the Library of Congress. Although not arranged for easy topical use and are not indexed, they remain the best compilation of information available for the study of the issues about electing the president of the United States. Reference has been made to the Hearings in the text of this work and the full citations will appear where needed. Additional information from the House and Senate Committees on the Judiciary are in summary form and contained in each Committee's Report designed to accompany the Hearings. These are in summary form and unlike the poorly organized Hearings are designed to present the issues and in readily useful summary format.

Source material also included appropriate issues of the Congressional Record to reflect the debates in the House and Senate and the recorded votes.

A number of books and articles have been published on the subjects examined over the years. Those appearing in recent years have yielded such information and assistance and where directly used citations have been entered. For easy reference, however, the primary ones utilized include the following:

Bickel, Alexander. The New Age of Political Reform. New York: Harper and Row, 1968.

Burns, James Macgregor. The Deadlock of Democracy. Englewood Cliffs, N. J.: Prentice-Hall, 1965.

Corwin, Edward S. The President, Office and Powers. New York: New York University Press, 1957.

Key, V. O. Politics, Parties, and Pressure Groups. New York: Thomas Y. Crowell, 1964

_____. Southern Politics. New York: Random House, 1949.

Longley, Lawrence D., and Alan G. Braun. The Politics of Electoral College Reform. New Haven, Conn.: Yale University Press, 1975.

Matthews, Donald R., ed. <u>Perspectives</u> on <u>Presidential</u>
<u>Selection</u>. Washington: Brookings Institution,
1973.

Michener, James A. <u>Presidential</u> <u>Lottery</u>. New York:
Random House, 1969.

Peirce, Neal R. and Lawrence D. Longley. <u>The</u> <u>People's</u>
<u>President</u>: <u>The</u> <u>Electoral</u> <u>College</u> in <u>American</u>
<u>History</u> and <u>the</u> <u>Direct</u> <u>Vote</u> <u>Alternative</u>. New
Haven: Yale University Press, rev. ed., 1981.

Petersen, Svend. <u>A</u> <u>Statistical</u> <u>History</u> <u>of</u> <u>the</u> <u>American</u>
<u>Presidential</u> <u>Elections</u>. New York: Ungar, 1968.

Phillips, Kevin P. <u>The</u> <u>Emerging</u> <u>Republican</u> <u>Majority</u>.
New Rochelle, N. Y.: Arlington House, 1969.

Rossiter, Clinton. <u>The</u> <u>American</u> <u>Presidency</u>. New York:
New American Library, 1964.

Sayre, Wallace S. and Judith H. Parris. <u>Voting</u> <u>for</u>
<u>President</u>: <u>The</u> <u>Electoral</u> <u>College</u> <u>and</u> <u>the</u> <u>American</u>
<u>Political</u> <u>System</u>. Washington: Brookings
Institution, 1972.

Sindler, Allan P., ed. <u>Policy</u> and <u>Politics</u> in <u>America-</u>
<u>-Six</u> <u>Case</u> <u>Studies</u>. Boston: Little, Brown and
Company, 1973.

White, Theodore H. <u>The</u> <u>Making</u> <u>of</u> <u>the</u> <u>President</u>, <u>1960</u>.
New York: New American Library, 1967.

_____, <u>The</u> <u>Making</u> <u>of</u> <u>the</u> <u>President</u>, 1968. New
York: Atheneum, 1969.

Wilmerding, Lucius. <u>The</u> <u>Electoral</u> <u>College</u>. New
Brunswick, N. J.: Rutgers University Press, 1958.

Zeidenstein, Harvey. <u>Direct</u> <u>Election</u> <u>of</u> <u>the</u> <u>President</u>.
Lexington, Mass.: Heath, 1973.

Pamphlets

American Enterprise Institute for Public Policy
     Research. Direct Election of the President.
     Washington: American Enterprise Institute for
     Public Policy Research, 1977.

Diamond, Martin. The Electoral College and the
     American Idea of Democracy. Washington: American
     Enterprise Institute for Public Policy Research,
     1977.

Articles

Banzhaf, John F., III. "One Man, 3.312 Votes: A
     Mathematical Analysis of the Electoral College."
     Villanova Law Review 13(Winter 1968), 303.

Bickel, Alexander. "The case for the Electoral
     College." New Republic 156(Jan. 28, 1967), 15.

Cronin, Thomas E. "The Direct Vote and the Electoral
     college: The Case for Meshing Things." Presiden-
     tial Studies Quarterly 9(Spring 1979), 144.

Eshleman, Kenneth. "Affirmative Gerrymandering is a
     matter of Justice." National Civic Review
     69(December 1980), 608.

Huitt, Ralph K. "The Congressional Committee: A Case
     Study." The American Political Science Review
     48(June 1954), 340.

Joyner, Conrad, and Ronald Pedderson. "The Electoral
     College Revisited." Southwestern Social Science
     Quarterly 45(June 1964), 26.

Kallenbach, Joseph. "Our Electoral College Gerry-
     mander." Midwest Journal of Political Science
     4(1960), 162.

Kirby, James C., Jr. "Limitations on the Power of
     State Legislatures over Presidential Elections."
     Law and Contemporary Problems 27(1962), 495.

Pomper, Gerald. "The Southern 'Free Elector' plan."
     Southwestern Social Science Quarterly 45(June
     1964), 478.

"State Power to Bind Presidential Electors." <u>Columbia</u>
<u>Law</u> <u>Review</u> 65(1965), 696.

Uslander, Eric M. "The Electoral College's Alma Mater
Should be a Swan Song." <u>Presidential</u> <u>Studies</u>
<u>Quarterly</u> 10(Summer 1980), 483.

Wells, David I. "Electing the President: How it Should
be Done." <u>National</u> <u>Civic</u> <u>Review</u> 66(May 1977),
230.

Wroth, L. Kinvin. "Election Contests and the Electoral
Vote." <u>Dickinson</u> <u>Law</u> <u>Review</u> 65(1961), 321.

The Direct National Popular Vote Proposal

Senate Joint Resolution 28 was the vehicle for the primary focus in the 1979 hearings before the Senate Committee on the Judiciary. It is reproduced here for reader reference. Following it is an explanatory commentary which was included in the Committee Report.

Senate Joint Resolution 28

Proposing an amendment to the Constitution to provide for the direct popular election of the President of the United States.

Resolved by the Senate and House of Representatives of the United States of America in Congress assembled (two-thirds of each House concurring therein), that the following article is proposed as an amendment to the Constitution of the United States, which shall be valid to all intents and purposes as part of the Constitution when ratified by the legislatures of three-fourths of the several states within seven years from the date of its submission by the Congress:

Article

Section 1. The people of the several States and the District constituting the seat of government of the United States shall elect the President and Vice President. Each elector shall cast a single vote for two persons who shall have consented to the joining of their names as candidates for the offices of President and Vice President. No candidate shall consent to the joinder of his name with that of more than one other person.

Section 2. The electors of President and Vice President in each State shall have the qualifications requisite for electors of the most numerous branch of the State legislature, except that for electors of President and Vice President the legislature of any State may prescribe less restrictive residence qualifications and for electors of President and Vice President the Congress may establish uniform residence qualifications.

Section 3. The persons joined as candidates for President and Vice President having the greatest number of votes shall be elected President and Vice President, if such number be at least 40 per centum of the whole number of votes cast.

If, after any such election, none of the persons joined as candidates for President and Vice President is elected pursuant to the preceeding paragraph, a runoff election shall be held in which the choice of President and Vice President shall be made from the two pairs of persons joined as candidates for President and Vice President who received the highest numbers of votes cast in the election. The pair of persons joined as candidates for President and Vice President receiving the greatest number of votes in such runoff shall be elected President and Vice President.

Section 4. The times, places, and manner of holding such elections and entitlement to inclusion on the ballot shall be prescribed in each State by the legislature thereof: but the Congress may at any time by law make or alter such regulations. The days for such elections shall be determined by Congress and shall be uniform throughout the United States. The Congress shall prescribe by law the times, places, and manner in which the results of such elections shall be ascertained and declared. No such election, other than a runoff election, shall be held later than the first Tuesday after the first Monday in November, and the results thereof shall be declared no later than the thirtieth day after the date on which the election occurs.

Section 5. The Congress may by law provide for the case of the death, inability, or withdrawal of any candidate for President or Vice President before a President and Vice President have been elected, and for the case of the death of both the President-elect and Vice President-elect.

Section 6. Sections 1 through 4 of this article shall take effect two years after the ratification of this article.

Section 7. The Congress shall have power to enforce this article by appropriate legislation.

Analysis of the Resolution

The resolution contains the customary provisions that the proposed new article to the Constitution shall

142

be valid as part of the Constitution only if ratified
by the legislatures of three-fourths of the States
within 7 years after it has been submitted to them by
the Congress.

Section 1 of the proposed article would abolish
the electoral college system of electing the President
and Vice President of the United States and provide
for their election by direct popular vote. The people
of every State and the District of Columbia would vote
directly for President and Vice President. This section prevents a candidate for either office from being
paired with more than one other person. Candidates
must consent to run jointly.

Section 2 provides that voters for President and
Vice President in each State must meet the qualifications for voting for the most numerous branch of the
State legislature in that State. The term "electors"
is retained, but instead of referring to the electoral
college, the term henceforth means qualified voters,
as it does in existing provisions dealing with popular
election of Members of Congress. This clause also
permits the legislature of any state to prescribe less
restrictive residence requirements and is necessary in
order to prevent invalidation of relaxed residence
requirements already or thereafter adopted by the
States for voting in Presidential elections.

The Congress is also empowered to establish
uniform residence qualifications. This authority
would in no way affect the provisions dealing with
residency requirements in Presidential elections
adopted as part of the Voting Rights Act of 1970. The
District of Columbia is not referred to in section 2
because Congress now possesses the legislative power
to establish voting qualifications for the District
under article I, section 8, clauses 17 and 18.

Section 2 is modeled after the provisions of
Article I, section 2, and the 17th amendment to the
Constitution regarding the qualifications of those
voting for Members of Congress. As a result, general
uniformity within each State regarding the qualifications for voting for all elected Federal officials is
retained. Use of the expression "electors of the most
numerous branch of the State legislature" does not
nullify by implication or intent the provisions of the
24th amendment that bar payment of a poll tax or any
other tax as a requisite for voting in Federal elections. The Supreme Court, moreover, has held that a

143

poll tax may not be enacted as a requisite for voting in State elections as well. Harper v. Board of Supervisors, 383 U.S. 663 (1966).

Section 3 requires that candidates obtain at least 40 percent of the whole number of votes cast to be elected President and Vice President. The expression "whole number of votes cast" refers to all valid votes counted in the final tally. Section 3 further provides that if no pair of persons receives at least 40 percent of the whole number of votes cast for President and Vice President, a popular runoff will be held among the two pairs of persons who receive the highest number of votes.

Section 4 embodies provisions imposing duties upon Congress and the States in regard to the conduct of elections. The first part of this section requires the State legislatures to prescribe the time, place, and manner of holding Presidential elections and entitlement to inclusion on the ballot--subject to a reserve power in Congress to make or alter such regulations. This provision is modeled after similar provisions in article I and the 17th amendment dealing with elections of members of Congress. States will continue to have the primary responsibility for regulating the ballot. However, if a State sought to exclude a major party candidate from appearing on the ballot-- as happened in 1948 and 1964--the Congress would be empowered to deal with such a situation.

Section 4 also requires Congress to establish by statute the days for the regular election and any runoff election, which must be uniform throughout the United States. This conforms to the present constitutional requirement for electoral voting (article II, section 1), to which Congress has responded by establishing a uniform day for the election of electors (3 U.S.C. 1).

Section 4 further requires Congress to prescribe the time, place and manner in which the results of such election shall be ascertained and declared. The mandatory language is comparable to the mandatory duties imposed upon the States to provide popular election machinery for Members of Congress. In implementing this section, Congress may choose to accept State certifications of the popular vote as it now accepts electoral State certifications under the provisions of 3 U.S.C 15. Federal enabling legislation will be required to provide the specific legislative details contemplated in the broad constitutional language of the amendment.

Section 5 empowers Congress to provide by legislation for the death, inability, or withdrawal of any candidate for President and Vice President either before or after a regular runoff election, but before a President or Vice President has been elected. Once a President and Vice President have been elected, existing constitutional provisions would apply. Thus, the death of the President-elect would be governed by the 20th amendment and the death of the Vice President-elect would be governed by the procedure for filling a Vice Presidential vacancy contained in the 25th amendment. Section 5 also empowers the Congress to provide by legislation for the case of the death of both the President-elect and Vice President-elect.

Section 6 provides that the article shall take effect 2 years after ratification. Since State and Federal legislation will be necessary fully to implement and effectuate the purposes of the proposed amendment, a reasonable period of time should be provided between the date of ratification and the date on which the amendment is to take effect.

Section 7 confers on Congress the power to enforce this article by appropriate legislation. The power conferred upon Congress by this section parallels the reserve power granted to the Congress by numerous amendments to the Constitution. Any exercise of power under this section must not only be "appropriate" to the effectuation of the article but must also be consistent with the Constitution.

The following is the text of a resolution to provide for a proportional plan for electing the president. It is typical of most which have been advanced in recent years.

JOINT RESOLUTION

Resolved by the Senate and House of Representatives of the United States of America in Congress assembled (two-thirds of each House concurring therein), That the following article is proposed as an amendment to the Constitution of the United States, which shall be valid to all intents and purposes as part of the Constitution only if ratified by three-fourths of the legislatures of the several States within seven years from the date of its submission by the Congress:

Section 1. The executive power shall be vested in a President of the United States of America. He shall hold his office during the term of four years, and, together with the Vice President, chosen for the same term, be elected as provided in this Constitution.

The office of elector of the President and Vice President, as established by section 1 of article II of this Constitution and the twelfth and twenty-third articles of amendment to this Constitution is hereby abolished. The President and Vice President shall be elected by the people of the several states and the district constituting the seat of government of the United States. The electors in each State shall have the qualifications requisite for electors of the most numerous branch of the State legislature, except that the legislature of any State may prescribe lesser qualifications with respect to residence therein. The electors in such district shall have such qualifications as the Congress may prescribe. The places and manner of holding such election in each State shall be prescribed by the legislature thereof; but the Congress may at any time by law make or alter such regulations. The place and manner of holding such election in such district shall be prescribed by the Congress. Congress shall determine the time of such election, which shall be the same throughout the United States. Until otherwise determined by the Congress, such election shall be held on the Tuesday next after the first Monday in November of the year preceding the year in which the regular term of the President is to begin. Each State shall be entitled

146

to a number of electoral votes equal to the whole
number of Senators and Representatives to which such
State may be entitled in the Congress. Such district
shall be entitled to a number of electoral votes equal
to the whole number of Senators and Representatives in
Congress to which such district would be entitled if
it were a State, but in no event more than the least
populous State.

Within forty-five days after such election, or
at such time as Congress shall direct, the official
custodian of the election returns of each State
and such district shall make distinct lists of all
persons for whom votes were cast for President and the
number of votes for each, and the total vote of the
electors of the State or the district for all persons
for President, which lists he shall sign and certify
and transmit sealed to the seat of the Government of
the United States, directed to the President of the
Senate. On the 6th day of January following the election, unless the Congress by law appoints a different
day not earlier than the 4th day of January and not
later than the 10th day of January, the President of
the Senate shall, in the presence of the Senate and
House of Representatives, open all certificates and
the votes shall then be counted. Each person for whom
votes were cast for President in each State and such
district shall be credited with such proportion of
the electoral votes thereof as he received of the
total vote of the electors therein for President. In
making the computation, fractional numbers less than
one one-thousandth shall be disregarded. The person
having the greatest number of electoral votes for
President shall be President, if such number be at
least 40 per centum of the whole number of such electoral votes. If no person has received at least 40
per centum of the whole number of electoral votes, or
if two persons have received an identical number of
electoral votes which is at least 40 per centum of the
whole number of electoral votes, then from the persons
having the two greatest numbers of electoral votes for
President, the Senate and the House of Representatives
sitting in joint session shall choose immediately, by
ballot, the President. A majority of the votes of
the combined authorized membership of the Senate and
the House of Representatives shall be necessary for a
choice.

The Vice President shall be likewise elected, at
the same time and in the same manner and subject to
the same provisions, as the President, but no person

constitutionally ineligible for the office of President shall be eligible to that of Vice President of the United States.

The Congress may by law provide for the case of the death of any of the persons from whom the Senate and the House of Representatives may choose a President whenever the right of choice shall have devolved upon them, and for the case of the death of any of the persons from whom the Senate and House of Representatives may choose a Vice President whenever the right of choice shall have devolved upon them. The Congress shall have power to enforce this article by appropriate legislation.

This article shall take effect on the 10th day of February next after one year shall have elapsed following its ratification.

The following is the text of a proposal for the district plan for electing the President and Vice-President. It is representative of those advanced in recent years.

JOINT RESOLUTION

Resolved by the Senate and House of Representatives of the United States of America in Congress assembled (two-thirds of each House concurring therein), That the following article is proposed as an amendment to the Constitution of the United States which shall be valid to all intents and purposes as part of the Constitution if ratified by the legislatures of three-fourths of the several States within seven years from the date of its submission by the Congress:

Section 1. Each State shall choose a number of electors of President and Vice President equal to the whole number of Senators and Representatives to which the State may be entitled in the Congress; but no Senator or Representative, or person holding an office of trust or profit under the United States, shall be chosen an elector.

The electors assigned to each State with its Senators shall be elected by the people thereof. Each of the electors apportioned with its Representatives shall be elected by the people of a single-member electoral district formed by the legislature of the State. Electoral districts within each State shall be of compact and contiguous territory containing substantially equal numbers of inhabitants, and shall not be altered until another census of the United States has been taken. Each candidate for the office of elector of President and Vice President shall file in writing under oath a declaration of the identity of the persons for whom he will vote for President and Vice President, which declaration shall be binding upon any successor to his office. In choosing electors the voters in each State shall have the qualifications requisite for electors of the most numberous branch of the State legislature.

The electors shall meet in their respective States, fill any vacancies in their number as directed by the State legislature, and vote by signed ballot for President and Vice President, one of whom, at least, shall not be an inhabitant of the same State with themselves; and they shall name in their ballots the person voted for as President, and in distinct ballots the person voted for as Vice President; and they shall make distinct lists of all persons voted for as President, and of all persons voted for as Vice President, the number of votes for each, and the name and electoral district, if any, of each elector who cast his vote for each such person, which lists they shall sign and certify, and transmit sealed to the seat of government of the United States, directed to the President of the Senate. The President of the Senate shall, in the presence of the Senate and the House of Representatives, open all the certificates and the votes shall then be counted. Any vote cast by an elector contrary to the declaration made by him shall be counted as a vote cast in accordance with his declaration. The person having the greatest number of electoral votes for President shall be the President, and the person having the greatest number of electoral votes for Vice President shall be the Vice President, if such numbers are a majority of the whole number of electors chosen. If two persons have the same total number of electoral votes, which number is one-half of the whole number of electors chosen, the person having the greatest number of votes cast by electors chosen from electoral districts shall be President, or Vice President, as the case may be.

If no person voted for as President has such a majority, then from the persons having the three highest numbers of votes for President, the Senate and House of Representatives together, each member having one vote, shall choose immediately, by ballot, the President. A quorum for such purpose shall be three-fourths of the whole number of the Senators and Representatives, and a majority of the whole number shall be necessary to a choice. If an additional ballot is necessary, the choice on the second ballot shall be between the two persons having the highest numbers of votes on the first ballot.

If no person voted for as Vice President has such a majority, then the Vice President shall be chosen from the persons having the three highest numbers of votes for Vice President in the same manner as herein provided for choosing the President. But no person constitutionally ineligible to the office of President shall be eligible to that of Vice President of the United States.

The Congress shall have power to carry this

article into effect by appropriate legislation. The Congress may provide by law for the determination of questions concerning breach of faith by electors in the casting of electoral votes, and for the case of the death of any of the persons from whom the Senate and the House of Representatives may choose a President or a Vice President whenever the right of choice shall have devolved upon them.

This article supersedes the second and third paragraphs of section 1, article II, of the Constitution, the twelfth article of amendment to the Constitution, and second 4 of the twentieth article of amendment to the Constitution.

Electors appointed pursuant to the twenty-third article of amendment to this Constitution shall be elected by the people of such district in such manner as the Congress may direct. Candidates for elector and electors of such district shall have the same obligations, and shall perform the same duties, as candidates for elector and electors of the several States under this article.

This article shall take effect on the 4th day of July following its ratification.

Index

154

About the Author

Adam C. Breckenridge is Professor Emeritus of political science, University of Nebraska-Lincoln, where he has served as a member of the faculty since 1946. He also held several administrative assignments in the University, including departmental chairman, Vice Chancellor for Academic Affairs, Acting Director of Libraries, and Interim Chancellor. A native of Missouri, he holds the Ph.D. in politics from Princeton University.

He is author of One House for Two: Nebraska's Unicameral Legislature, The Right to Privacy, Congress Against the Court, and The Executive Privilege.